I0427907

Table of Contents

Introduction

China is a country on the rise with an emerging economy and growing military capability that grant it world power status. It has a permanent seat on the United Nations' Security Council, nuclear weapons, one of the world's largest populations, and a communist form of government. Of concern to the West is China's expansionist development in spite of their stated desire for a harmonious world order. This expansion has the potential for future conflict whether it is economic or military in nature. It is therefore critical that the West understands Chinese culture. To do this, the West needs to understand how China perceives issues they deem important. Knowing this could help defuse potentially dangerous situations. The purpose of this monograph is to understand how China's culture affects the way it behaves internationally. The goal of this research is to identify and articulate Chinese behavioral characteristics that may be useful to predict future relations with the United States.

This study is based on my premise that countries act based on their past experiences and how they perceive reality. Their perception of reality is filtered through the lens of their values and beliefs. Together, a country's past experiences (history) and beliefs (predominant philosophies) make up a cultural lens through which a country perceives reality. Therefore, understanding the Chinese cultural lens might enable one to anticipate expected Chinese behavior that could impact relations with international actors.

Part one of this monograph reviews Chinese culture and sketches how China perceives itself. In order to understand Chinese culture, this study examines two key aspects about China's past: influential philosophies and formative events in its recent history (defined as the last 200 years). The review of philosophies shows how Chinese view these beliefs as inclusive rather than exclusive. China's secular and Legalist traditions contributed to the adoption of communism in the twentieth century. Examining Confucianism shows how the appreciation for harmony, an established hierarchy, and an emphasis on education are still prevalent today. The review of Daoism illustrates the influence of two important aspects—constant change (*ying-yang*) and the concept of letting the situation develop (*wu-wei*). The review of Chinese strategic thought highlights three important aspects from Sun Tzu: knowing self, setting conditions, and developing the situation. These are further illustrated through a review of the strategic board game *GO* which demonstrates the Chinese approach to warfighting and diplomacy. *GO* provides a marked contrast to the classic western European game of strategy—chess. All together, the issues of Chinese philosophies, history, and strategic thought provide the lens through which we may be able to perceive Chinese actions more clearly.

As a point of departure for historical events, this study begins with the Opium Wars. The Opium Wars mark the beginning of the Century of Humiliation for China when the West collided with China's view of the international system which drew on the legalist and Confucian tradition of China's classical civilization. This system of government evolved over centuries and enabled the Chinese civilization to develop into a sophisticated culture, which at times far surpassed the early civilizations of the West. China's geographic positioning in Asia and relative advancements in science and governance, compared to neighboring countries, led the Chinese to refer to themselves as the Middle Kingdom. When the British forced their way into China in the mid-1800s in order to gain access to new markets, the results were catastrophic: China's concept of their Middle Kingdom being a superior civilization was challenged; their Confucian-based form of imperial rule was weakened; their traditional means for dealing with barbarians (foreigners) proved inadequate; and despite early Chinese inventions, the West proved superior in the development of both their scientific and technological achievements. Worst of all, imperialist expansion resulted in the carving up China. This was most painfully demonstrated by Japan— a country smaller in size and considered inferior by the Chinese. The monograph continues to examine formative events in Chinese history through the establishment of the People's Republic of China (PRC), when Mao Zedong assumed power. Although some of Mao's later efforts to advance China actually had a reverse effect, he is at least credited with modernizing China during his rule—an achievement which his predecessors were unable to do in the century and multiple governments preceding his.

The second part of this study examines contemporary China's stated core interests and means to achieve their desired goals. China's core interests are to keep the Chinese Communist Party in power,

2

maintain its sovereignty, and sustain China's current levels of economic and social development. China's desired goal is to regain its position of power in the Pacific and overcome the stigma attached to the Century of Humiliation. This study focuses on China's efforts to energize its economy and modernize its military, both of which enabled China to reach its desired position in the international system.

The final part of this monograph reviews China's perception of the United States and suggests how the two countries might continue peaceful international relations in the future. China currently views any action in the Pacific by the United States as a means to contain China and prevent it from rising to its full potential. China's economic success over the last decade also allowed it to increase its efforts to modernize the military. Alarmists see this action as an attempt to establish a hegemony in the Pacific, while moderates see military modernization as a byproduct of economic growth. Regardless, both alarmists and moderates agree that the stakes are too high for the United States or China to miscalculate the other.

The key texts that informed this study can be divided into three categories: philosophy, history, and contemporary commentary and analysis. Regarding philosophy, a comparative look at Confucianism, Legalism, and Daoism proved useful in understanding Chinese philosophies. In the West, Sun Tzu writings are often viewed to be emblematic of the Chinese strategic way of thinking. Ralph D. Sawyer's translation of Sun Tzu's *Art of War* was particularly helpful in identifying the principle of the indirect approach and the need to set conditions for victory before acting. Francois Jullien highlights Daoist beliefs and applications in his book, *A Treatise on Efficacy: between Western and Chinese Thinking*. David Lai's article on the strategic board game *GO* helped illustrate these two traits and contrasted them against the Western direct approach and tendency to attack an objective using force-on-force. Mao Zedong's own treatise on guerilla warfare provided practical applications where these two strategic traits,

3

the indirect approach and setting the conditions for victory, were used against an actual enemy—Japan during World War Two.[1]

There are several historians from the twentieth century who are well respected in the field of Chinese history whose works proved helpful. The first is Harvard scholar John K. Fairbank and his book *The United States and China*. The second is Massachusetts Institute of Technology professor Lucian Pye and his book, *China: An Introduction*, which provides a comprehensive review of the Confucian period of Chinese history as well as the first twenty years of communist rule. The third historian is Yale professor Jonathan D. Spence who has written a detailed and comprehensive review of modern China. His book, *The Search for Modern China*, was most beneficial in setting the historical context of events as well as explaining the significance of the results. James E. Sheridan provides a thorough review of the Chinese Republican Era in his book, *China in Disintegration*, while Donald A. Jordan's book, *The Northern Expedition*, provides an in depth look at Chiang Kai-Shek's rise to power and the Nationalist Party's early attempts to unify China. Edgar Snow's book, *Red Star over China*, was first published in 1938 and provides one of the sympathetic, early western accounts of Mao Zedong and his Chinese communist leaders.[2] Together, these authors helped portray an accurate account of critical events in Chinese history during the last two hundred years.

---

[1] For general surveys on China, see Francois Jullien, *A Treatise on Efficacy: Between Western and Chinese Thinking* (Honolulu: University of Hawaii Press, 2004); David Lai, *Learning from the Stones: a GO Approach to Mastering China's Strategic Concept, Shi* (Carlisle Barracks: Strategic Studies Institute, May 2004); William H. Mott IV and Jae Chang Kim, *The Philosophy of Chinese Military Culture* (New York: Palgrave MacMillan, 2006); Ralph D. Sawyer, *Sun Tzu: The Art of War* (Boulder: Westview Press, 1994). Mao Zedong, *On Guerrilla Warfare*. Translated by Samuel B. Griffith II (Chicago: University of Illinois Press, 1961); Andrew Scobell, *China and Strategic Culture* (Carlisle Barracks: Strategic Studies Institute, May 2002).

[2] For sources that clarify specific periods in Chinese history, see John K. Fairbank, *The United States and China*, 4th ed. (Cambridge, Massachusetts: Harvard University Press, 1979); Donald A. Jordan, *The Northern Expedition: China's National Revolution of 1926-1928* (Honolulu: The University of Hawaii Press, 1976); Lucian Pye, *China: An Introduction* (Boston: Little, Brown and Company, 1972); James E. Sheridan, *China in Disintegration: The Republican Era in Chinese History, 1912-1949* (New York: The Free Press, A Division of Macmillan Publishing, 1975); Edgar Snow, *Red Star over China* (New York: Grove Press, 1961); Jonathan D. Spence, *The Search for Modern China* (New York: W. W. Norton and Company, 1990).

Growing interest in and concern towards China's relation to the international system has contributed to a very considerable volume of contemporary literature on China. Analysis on China's current capabilities and positions on international relations can be categorized into three broad areas: works by contemporary journalists and political scientists; written opinions by current and elder statesmen; and current government reports. Missouri State professor David Walgreen and Georgetown professor Robert G. Sutter have written extensively on China and proved insightful regarding China's recent rise to power and its influence in Asia as well as the Pacific. Journalist Robert D. Kaplan's book, *Monsoon*, is a concise and easy to read work on the geopolitical and geostrategic significance of the Indian Ocean and its significance to China. For a review of China's domestic concerns, Professor Jeffrey Wasserstrom provides a contemporary account of issues in his work *China in the 21st Century* and Susan L. Craig provides a review of perceived traditional and nontraditional security threats in her Strategic Studies Institute report. For an in depth look at the Chinese Communist Party, journalist Richard McGregor's book, *The Party: The Secret World of China's Communist Rulers*, is useful. While there are some who derive alarmist views on the threat of China's rapid rise to power, such as Steven W. Mosher's book, *Hegemon: China's Plan to Dominate Asia and the World*, and Colonels Qiao Liang and Wang Xiangsui's book, *Unrestricted Warfare: China's Master Plan to Destroy America*;[3] current Secretary of State Hillary Clinton's November article, "America's Pacific Century," in *Foreign Policy* magazine, describes a more pragmatic and balanced course for the United States on which to proceed in the Pacific. Both former Secretary of State, Henry Kissinger, and former National Security Advisor, Zbigniew Bzrezinski have also recently published recent works that caution the United States against miscalculating China's rise to power.[4] They also encourage the United States to remain actively engaged with China

---

[3] For alarmist views, see Colonel Qiao Liang and Colonel Wang Xiangsui, *Unrestricted Warfare: China's Master Plan to Destroy America* (Panama City, Panama: Pan American Publishing Company, 2002); and Steven W. Mosher, *Hegemon: China's Plan to Dominate Asia and the World* (San Francisco: Encounter Books, 2000).

[4] For moderate and pragmatic views, see Hillary Clinton, "America's Pacific Century," *Foreign Policy* (November 2011): 56-63; Elizabeth Van Wie Davis, "Governance in China in 2010," *Asian Affairs: An American Review* (2009): 195-211; Robert D. Kaplan, *Monsoon: The Indian Ocean and the*

regarding areas of mutual interest. Current government reports, such as the 2011 Department of Defense *Annual Report to Congress on Military and Security Developments Involving the People's Republic of China,* and works published by the Congressional Research Service proved most helpful in providing an analysis of China's current military and economic capabilities. [5]

Chinese Culture

The two influential philosophies that are examined are Confucianism and Daoism. Confucianism was selected because of its major impact on the dynastic form of government. Daoism was selected based on its influence on China's strategic thought. Some notable Confucian concepts that are still prevalent today are: the desire to live in harmony, an appreciation for a hierarchical system, the government's endorsement of the importance of education, and rule by a strong centralized form of government. The review of Daoism will illustrate the concept of nature being in an ever-evolving state of change (*ying-yang*) and the concept of doing nothing (*wu-wei*) in order to let things develop before acting. Sun Tzu's *Art of War* and the ancient board game of strategic encirclement, *GO*, will be examined to illustrate the Daoist influence on strategic thinking. Together these will show the concepts of knowing oneself, developing the situation, and setting the conditions for victory before acting.

Future of American Power (New York: Random House, 2010); Ronald C. Keith. *China: From the Inside Out* (New York: Pluto Press, 2009); Kenneth Lieberthal. *Governing China: From Revolution to Reform, Second Edition* (New York: W. W. Norton and Company, 2004); Richard McGregor, *The Party: The Secret World of China's Communist Rulers* (New York: Harper Collins Publishers, 2010); David Shambaugh, *Modernizing China's Military* (Berkeley, California: University of California Press, 2002); Robert G. Sutter, *China's Rise in Asia* (Lanham, Maryland: Rowman and Littlefield Publishers, 2005); David Walgreen, "China in the Indian Ocean Region: Lessons in PRC Grand Strategy," *Comparative Strategy* (2006): 55-73; and Jeffrey N. Wasserstrom, *China in the 21ˢᵗ Century* (New York: Oxford University Press, 2010).

[5] For official government documents, see Department of Defense, "Annual Report to Congress on Military and Security Developments Involving the People's Republic of China." Washington, D.C. (6 May 2011); Susan L. Craig, *Chinese Perceptions of Traditional and Nontraditional Security Threats* (Carlisle Barracks: Strategic Studies Institute, March 2007); and June Teufel Dreyer, *China's Strategic View: The Role of the People's Liberation Army* (Carlisle Barracks: Strategic Studies Institute, April 1996).

Influential Philosophies.

Outside the realm of the world's monotheistic religions, syncretic practices are common. In the East, instead of the common Western perspective of a religion being exclusive (for example, Judaism, Christianity, and Islam are all monotheistic and espouse that there is no other god), there is more of a sense of a melding of religions in order to achieve a balance of harmony. As such, the major religions of the East, Buddhism, Confucianism, and Daoism, along with various cults, are seen as interrelated and complementary, rather than exclusive. Of the numerous religions and philosophies in China, Confucianism, Legalism, and Daoism still influence Chinese thinking today. [6]

Confucianism is based off the teachings of the Chinese philosopher and teacher Kongfuzi who lived between 551-479 B.C. (His anglicized name was translated as Confucius.) He developed his philosophy during the Warring States period in Chinese history with the goal of bringing peace and harmony to the people. Confucius taught that in order to live in harmony one must practice righteousness and restraint. One should study the Five Classics (*The Book of Rites [Li Ji], Spring and Autumn Annals [Chun Qiu], The Book of History [Shu Ji], The Book of Poetry [Shi Ji],* and *The Book of Changes [Yi Jing]*), worship one's ancestors, and show due deference to authority. His teachings were based on a code of good behavior which was recorded in the Four Books: *Analects, Mencius, the Doctrine of the Mean,* and *The Great Learning.* [7] The *Analects* stress the importance of education, ritual, and relationships that are hierarchical but yet beneficial to both superior and subordinate.[8] Confucius believed it was through education that one could improve one's position in life and learn from history. Ritual was important because this is how one remembered the best practices from the past. Hierarchical relationships were stressed with an emphasis placed on knowing the responsibilities at each level, for example the relationship between the ruler and his subject, a father and his son, etc. This philosophy, stressing

---

[6] John L. Esposito, Darrell J. Fasching, and Todd Lewis, *World Religions Today* (Oxford: Oxford University Press, 2002), 432.

[7] Spence, *The Search for Modern China,* 791.

[8] Wasserstrom, *China in the 21st Century,* 2.

hierarchical relationships and the propriety of rituals, fit well with imperial Chinese dynasties as it was commonly believed that the emperors were the Sons of Heaven and ruled by Heavenly Mandate. During the Han dynasty (206 B.C.-222 A.D.), Confucianism was adopted as the state religion and continued to play a predominant role in both government and society for the next two millennia.

However in the early 1900s, following decades of domestic upheaval and foreign intervention, several Chinese intellectuals argued against the teachings of Confucius and blamed the country's troubles on this philosophy. Historian Lucian Pye noted,

> Confucianism was remarkable because it was secular and was considered valid and appropriate for the problems of everyone, whether emperor, bureaucrat, gentry, or ordinary subject…The Confucian ideal was eminently appropriate for an agrarian society but was detrimental to the development of commerce and industry.[9]

Western powers with advanced scientific and military technology were able to force their way into China and establish treaty ports to enhance their trade and economy. The inability of the Chinese dynasty (that was based on Confucian ideals) to deal effectively with foreigners was brought into question. These cognitive tensions fed directly into the Chinese Revolution of 1911and the ultimate downfall of the Qing dynasty. Historian Jeffry Wasserstrom described the concerns of the intellectual elite and scholars in the following manner, "To join the modern world, they claimed, China needed to jettison Confucius and everything that he represented, embracing the best that the West had to offer as, they claimed, Japan had done—resulting in its rising global influence."[10] In fact, during the later years of the Maoist era (1949-1976), Confucius was portrayed as a man whose anti-egalitarian ideas had caused great harm to several generations of both Chinese men and women. The concept of viewing females as less value than males was singled out as potentially harmful to future generations. Ironically, the Chinese Communist Party (CCP) has since reversed its anti-Confucius position and now emphasizes continuity with the past,

---

[9] Pye, *China: An Introduction*, 32.
[10] Wasserstrom, *China in the 21ˢᵗ Century*, 9.

especially ideas and practices that suggest greatness or harmonious relationships.[11] In modern China, Confucianism is currently experiencing a rebirth. According to religious scholar, John Esposito:

> Confucianism has been reanalyzed in positive terms: family-based businesses are efficient in maximizing scarce capital; tightly woven kin/family relations are excellent building blocks for supply and product distribution; an education system that fostered group cooperation, memorization, and imitation has proven adept at producing individuals able to master existing technologies and make them remarkably better. [12]

As an influential philosophy, Confucianism clearly left a lasting impact on China, its strongest influence being felt during the last dynasties from 200 B.C. to 1911. The desire for harmony, respect for education, ritual, and a strong centralized government / figure head can all be attributed to this ancient way of thinking and are still prevalent today.

The Legalist school of thought espoused that the only way to deal with the chaotic problems of the Warring States Period was to establish and enforce the authority of a legal system. As historian Lucian Pye noted, "The Legalists argued that the problems of the day could be readily swept away if the ruler would establish clear and unambiguous laws and strictly enforce them."[13] The Legalists believed that once the Chinese saw the violators of the law dealt with swiftly and harshly, order and tranquility would resume.

Lord Shang (Shang Yang), the Prime Minister of the state of Chin, is credited with adopting the Legalist theories of Han Fei-tzu and putting them into practice. Lord Shang was further able to convince his ruler, Chin Shih Huang-ti, that together with the ruler's military expertise and enforcement of the Legalist system, China could be united. He was correct and China was united in 221 B.C. with Chin Shih Huang-ti becoming the first emperor. Many of Lord Shang's legalistic practices eventually evolved into bureaucratic laws. Lord Shang and the Legalists emphasized that the head of the state held special authority and his decisions must have the respect and the obedience of the people. This reinforced the Legalist notion of the primacy of the state over the individual. Unfortunately for Lord Shang, he did not survive the passing of Emperor Chin Shih Huang-ti. This was partially due to Lord Shang's strict

---

[11] Ibid., 13.

[12] Esposito, *World Religions Today*, 436.

[13] Pye, *China: An Introduction*, 135.

enforcement of the law and also because of the fact Lord Shang offended the emperor's son. When the son assumed power, he had Lord Shang put to death.

Although, Confucianism was later adopted as the state ideology, the Legalists left their mark on Chinese society. The concept that the head of state retains absolute authority and that the state has primacy over the individual is still followed today. This may also explain how Mao Zedong was able to establish himself absolute ruler over China with a communist form of government that sacrificed the needs of the individual for the good of the state.

Daoism was introduced in China around 600 B.C. by Lao Zi. His philosophy proposed an alternative to Confucianism whereby he believed harmony would only be achieved if "humanity had synchronized itself with nature and the *Dao*, the mystical reality underlying it."[14] *Dao* was considered the "prime source of creation, from which the *yin* and *yang* forces emerge in ever-shifting harmonies."[15] *Yin* represented the dark, earth, female, autumn, valley, west, and *Po* soul (grave) forces of nature. *Yang* represented the bright, heaven, male, spring, mountain, east, and *Hun* soul (heaven) forces of nature. Followers of Daoism considered the universe in a constantly changing status and, as such, graphically depicted the *yin-yang* symbol as two interlocking tear-drop shaped S-curves, opposing each other, within a circle.[16] The first beliefs of *Dao* are considered to have been written in the *Daodejing* (*Tao Te Ching*) by Lao Zi. However, he paradoxically stated that true *Dao* "cannot be spoken or adequately defined."[17] Lao Zi also described a way of noninterference (*wu-wei*) which he summed up in the saying, "do nothing and nothing will be left undone." Because *wu-wei* is intentionally vague, this may be interpreted as letting nature take its course, the art of doing nothing, or simply going with the flow. The *Daodejing* also uses water as an analogy whereby water flows "with the natural forces and circumstances, yet can

---

[14] Esposito, *World Religions Today*, 444.
[15] Ibid.
[16] Ibid., 447.
[17] Ibid., 444.

overcome all obstacles."[18] The Daoist ideas of harmony, *yin-yang*, *wu-wei*, and the analogy of water resonate throughout Chinese culture and also appear in their strategic concepts.

The French professor of Chinese studies, Francois Jullien, has highlighted these Daoist beliefs and applications in his book, *A Treatise on Efficacy: between Western and Chinese Thinking.* The book notes the differences between the Western and Chinese concepts of time, patience, and use of the indirect approach—allowing the situation to evolve until the right conditions exist before acting. He writes, "in China, we discover a concept of efficacy that teaches one to learn how to allow an effect to come about: not to aim for it (directly) but to implicate it (as a consequence)… not to seek it, but simply to welcome it—to allow it to result."[19] Jullien also identifies one of the keys to Chinese strategy as relying on the "inherent potential (*shi*)" of the situation and to be "carried along as it evolves."[20] He states that success comes to those who are able to adapt to the situation in order to profit from it, rather than following a predetermined, ideal model. [21] In Chapter Six, titled "Do Nothing (with Nothing Left Undone)," he explains why the dragon is often used by the Chinese as an analogy of a state of constant evolution:

> The dragon's flexible body has no fixed form; it weaves and bends in every direction, contracting in order to deploy itself, coiling up in order to progress. It merges so closely with the clouds that, borne constantly along by them, it advances without the slightest of effort. Its movement is hardly distinguishable from that of the clouds. In the same way, strategic intentionality should have no fixed goal, is fixed on no particular plan, and so can adapt to every twist in the situation and profit from it.[22]

Jullien's examples clearly reflect a Daoist influence in Chinese thought, especially with regard to a constantly changing situation (*yin-yang*) and letting the situation develop (*wu-wei*) before one acts.

Strategic Thought.

In his book, *On China*, Henry Kissinger states, "The Chinese have been shrewd practitioners of *Realpolitik* and students of strategic doctrine distinctly different from the strategy and diplomacy that found favor in the West." Where the West has focused on a single decisive clash or battle to resolve

---

[18] Ibid.
[19] Jullien, *A Treatise on Efficacy*, vii.
[20] Ibid., 20.
[21] Ibid., 26.
[22] Ibid., 97.

differences, the Chinese "stressed subtlety, indirection, and the patient accumulation of relative advantage."[23] Sun Tzu's treatise on ancient Chinese warfare titled, *The Art of War,* illustrate these traits. Sun Tzu was an imperial advisor who lived around 500 B.C. and made his living by traveling from one Chinese king, or warlord, to the next selling military advice. The American scholar and historian of ancient Chinese warfare, Ralph D. Sawyer, has written a helpful interpretation of Sun Tzu's manuscript which reveals several parallels to the Daoist school of thought. Sawyer also highlights additional Chinese perspectives on warfare that at times differ with traditional Western thinking. There are three broad categorizations that summarize Sun Tzu's strategic advice: know yourself and the enemy; set the conditions for victory through imbalance and deception; and be patient and let the situation develop.

In today's parlance, we would describe knowing yourself and the enemy as having not just situational awareness, but rather having a more complete picture or situational understanding. Sun Tzu described this condition the following way:

> Thus it is said that the one who knows the enemy and knows himself will not be endangered in a hundred engagements. One who does not know the enemy but knows himself will sometimes be victorious, sometimes meet with defeat. One who knows neither the enemy nor himself will invariably be defeated in every engagement.[24]

Once situational understanding was achieved, Sun Tzu realized that the conditions for victory could be manipulated through timing and imbalance. This concept of timing is better understood if one considers it in the context of 'tactical patience' or knowing when the conditions are right to attack. Sun Tzu wrote,

> In antiquity those that excelled in warfare first made themselves unconquerable in order to await [the moment when] the enemy could be conquered...the victorious army first realizes the conditions for victory, and then seeks to engage in battle. The vanquished army fights first, and then seeks victory.[25]

Sun Tzu also advised the ruler to set the conditions for victory through imbalance and deception. "Warfare is the Way (Tao) of deception. Thus although [you are] capable, display incapability to them. When committed to employing your forces, feign inactivity. When [your objective] is nearby, make it

---

[23] Henry Kissinger, *On China* (New York: Penguin Press, 2011), 23.
[24] Sawyer, *Sun Tzu*, 179.
[25] Ibid., 184.

12

appear as if distant; when far away, create the illusion of being nearby."[26] Another way to achieve this imbalance was through the use of both orthodox and unorthodox forces. "What enables the masses of the Three Armies invariably to withstand the enemy without being defeated are the unorthodox (*ch'i*) and the orthodox (*cheng*)…in battle one engages with the orthodox and gains victory through the unorthodox."[27] We see this concept manifested today in Chinese military strategy with their emphasis being placed on asymmetric warfare as well as traditional symmetrical (industrialized) methods. This will be discussed in a later section.

Adaptability is another of Sun Tzu's keys to victory. Sun Tzu uses a water analogy to describe how an army might adapt itself to the conditions on the battlefield:

> Now the army's disposition of force (*hsing*) is like water. Water's configuration (*hsing*) avoids heights and races downward. The army's disposition of force (*hsing*) avoids the substantial and strikes the vacuous. Water configures (*hsing*) its flow in accord with the terrain; the army controls its victory in accord with the enemy. Thus the army does not maintain any constant strategic configuration of power (*shih*), water has no constant shape (*hsing*). One who is able to change and transform in accord with the enemy and wrest victory is termed spiritual. Thus [none of] the five phases constantly dominates; the four seasons do not have constant positions; the sun shines for longer and shorter periods; and the moon wanes and waxes.[28]

Sun Tzu's writings clearly reflect the influence of Daoist thought on Chinese strategic concepts. While *The Art of War* contains additional axioms than just those presented here, we see the familiar Daoist concepts of the water analogy and the constantly evolving balance of events (*yin-yang*). However, Sun Tzu expands these further by manipulating this balance through deception until conditions are favorable to his desires.

Chinese strategic concepts are also revealed in an ancient board game called *GO*. In 2004, political science professor David Lai addressed this topic in an article titled, "Learning from the Stones: A GO Approach to Mastering China's Strategic Concept, Shi." The basis behind writing this article was the perceived knowledge gap the United States has regarding the Chinese concept of "*shi*" (pronounce "sure"). *Shi* roughly translates as the "propensity" of an object. Professor Lai points out that this

---

[26] Ibid., 168.
[27] Ibid., 187.
[28] Ibid., 193.

concept of *shi* is not new, and there is even a chapter dedicated to the subject in Sun Tzu's classic work on martial strategy, *The Art of War*.[29] Professor Lai uses the ancient strategy game *GO* to explain the Chinese emphasis on strategy and stratagems.[30] He states, "This game bears a striking resemblance to the Chinese way of war and diplomacy. Its concepts and tactics are living reflections of Chinese philosophy, strategic thinking, stratagems, and tactical interactions."[31] Citing Sun Tzu, he points out that the Chinese are comfortable with the dialectic nature of things, very similar to the Daoist philosophy of *Yin* and *Yang*. Water is again used as an example of the dialectic nature of things.

> It (water) has no constant shape. There is nothing softer and weaker than water, yet nothing is more penetrating and capable of attacking the hard and the strong. The flow of water, carrying with it the shi, can wash away anything standing in its way.[32]

The game of *GO* is one of strategic encirclement. The object of the game is for the player to secure as many places (territory) on the board as possible. The square board represents the earth and its four corners represent the seasons. The game pieces (stones) are round and represent mobility. Since each player starts with 180 pieces, moving one stone at a time, the game slowly develops. In fact, the first 50 moves are considered "opening-stage" moves. Eventually the game becomes more complicated as each player tries to surround the opponent's pieces in order to force a withdrawal from a space or face capitulation. As such, "the competition for more territory thus leads to invasion, engagement, confrontation, and war fighting."[33] The game is basically one of strategic posturing and maneuvering, setting conditions to strike the opponent, but waiting for the right moment when the conditions are right. The winner of the game is usually not apparent until the very end of the game and often only wins by a small margin. The concept of who is attacking whom is sometimes a matter of perception. In the end, the winner is the player who controls the most territory.

---

[29] Lai, *Learning from the Stones*, 2. Note: In the Samuel B. Griffith translation of The Art of War, *shi* is translated to mean "energy."

[30] Ibid., 6. Note: *GO* is actually the Japanese name. The Chinese name is *WEI QI*

[31] Ibid., 2.

[32] Ibid., 4.

[33] Ibid., 8.

The game of *GO* is used in this study to demonstrate the Chinese approach to war fighting and diplomacy. It is a game of maneuvering and posturing to achieve a long term strategic end state. The successful player sets the conditions and waits patiently before he attacks his opponent. *GO* also provides a marked contrast to the popular Western game of strategy—chess. In chess, while a player may think several moves ahead, the game essentially boils down to a force-on-force confrontation. American football is another example where emphasis is placed on using brute force to achieve gains on the playing field. Consider these two games within the context of the German military theorist, Carl von Clausewitz, who wrote about attacking an opponent's center of gravity and defeating the enemy's Army as the key to victory.[34] This methodology is in stark contrast to Sun Tzu who advised using the indirect approach, avoiding the enemy's strengths, and attacking the enemy's strategy in order to defeat him. The player in *GO* must constantly watch the entire situation and cannot become fixated or focused on one object. While the chess player is focused on destroying the enemy and removing his pieces from the board, the *GO* player is focused on building or creating opportunities.

Formative Events in Chinese History

A review of the evolution of historical events in modern Chinese history explains why the period of 1839-1949 is considered by the Chinese as the Century of Humiliation. It is important to understand how the Chinese perception of the Century of Humiliation created the conditions for Chinese society to challenge the traditional norms of its civilization and experiment with the new ideologies of the twentieth century. Reviewing historical events explains how the Confucian-based form of government was inadequate for the modern world, how the West exploited China through imperialist expansion, and how Mao Zedong leveraged popular discontent and ultimately succeeded in dragging China into the twentieth century. This review also illuminates why China has an extreme distrust of foreigners, a strong desire to

---

[34] Carl von Clausewitz, *On War* translated and edited by Michael Howard and Peter Paret (New York: Alfred A. Knopf, 1984), 577.

15

reestablish itself as an internationally respected country, and why China places such a huge emphasis on modernizing both its military and economy.

Dynastic Period.

The Dynastic Period was a time when China was an advanced civilization, was respected by its neighbors, and had developed a form of government that was optimal for an agrarian society. All was well for the emperor as long as the status quo was maintained. This period dates as far back as 2000 B.C. beginning with the Hsia Dynasty, and ending in 1911 with the Qing Dynasty.[35] During the early portion of the dynastic period, China developed into a sophisticated culture, which at times far surpassed the early civilizations of the West. By the Qin Dynasty (221-206 B.C.), China had standardized weights and measures, minted bronze coins, and was building roads, canals, and the renowned Great Wall of China.[36] It was also during these earlier dynastic periods that the people of China believed their rulers had received a "Mandate from Heaven" to rule. As such, the emperors were considered "Sons of Heaven" and were expected to be wise and unselfish and rule on behalf of the people.[37] Historian Lucian Pye noted, "The moral theory of the dynastic cycle was encouraged by the concept of the Mandate of Heaven, by which emperors could legitimately rule so long as their conduct was consistent with the Will of Heaven."[38] The emperor held a special status as both a political figure and the intermediary with heaven. People believed that the emperors ruled by the consent of Heaven. If this consent was lost, then the dynastic cycle could be periodically broken by either rebels, foreign armies, or natural disasters that plagued the country.[39] During the Tang Dynasty (618-907 A.D.), China developed gun powder and wood block printing. This dynasty lasted for almost 300 years and was considered a golden age. China expanded as far east as

---

[35] Pye, *China: An Introduction*, 33.
[36] Earl Davies, *Encyclopedia of Discovery Science and History* (San Francisco: Fog City Press, 2002), 346.
[37] Ibid., 354.
[38] Pye, *China: An Introduction*, 54.
[39] Wasserstrom, *China in the 21ˢᵗ Century*, 21.

16

Korea, as far south as Vietnam, and towards Tibet in the west. Art, craft, music, and literature flourished and China traded with other countries, such as Persia, along the Silk Road.[40]

The early Chinese civilization was contained by significant terrain features that formed natural boundaries. The original Chinese established themselves in an area that was bounded by the Yellow River to the north, the Wei River to the northwest, and the Yangzi River in the south. The Taklamakan Desert was to the northwest, the Himalayan Mountains were to the southwest, and the Pacific Ocean was to the east. This Sinocentric view of the world has had a lasting impact on Chinese statecraft and helps explain why the Century of Humiliation was so striking to the Chinese mindset. The Chinese remained within these boundaries for centuries working the land and developing their own civilization. They were aware of other civilizations but did not feel compelled to deal with those less sophisticated. Hence, the Chinese referred to themselves as the "Middle Kingdom."[41] Within these natural boundaries, China knew of India and exchanged goods and religious beliefs (Buddhism) but remained content in their own Middle Kingdom.

While many in Europe were impressed with the Chinese government's organization and discipline, China's tributary system became a point of friction. The Sinocentric belief of superiority, suspicion of outsiders, and thought that other societies had little to offer China, except tribute, lasted into the late 1700s. China continued to spread its influence abroad by way of commerce and culture. Europeans found the Chinese secular form of government of interest and were impressed how, "virtuous conduct, in many ways adequate to Christian standards, could be achieved without revealed religion." [42] Voltaire's 1756 book, *Essay on Morals*, praised the Chinese for the concepts of order and discipline and some scholars even considered the Chinese superior in the practical organization of their society and

---

[40] Davies, *Encyclopedia of Discovery Science and History*, 350.
[41] Ibid., 342.
[42] Fairbank, *The United States and China*, 156. Note: the eighteenth century was also a time period when Chinese motifs became vogue not only in architecture and landscape gardening but also in artwork, furniture making, and ceramics.

administrative affairs. However, it was the concept of the Chinese tributary system where the Western

culture clashed with the East.

The Chinese felt, due to their superiority and imperial benevolence, that foreigners should submit

themselves before the emperor as sign of respect and pay tribute if they wished to conduct business. This

was the price of admission for a "barbarian into the civilization of the Middle Kingdom."[43] Foreign

envoys were expected to perform the ritual known as the kowtow. Fairbank states:

> The full kowtow was no mere prostration of the body but a prolonged series of three separate kneeling,
> each one leading to three successive prostrations, nose upon the floor. The "three kneeling and nine
> prostrations" left no doubt in anyone's mind, least of all in the performer's, as to who was inferior and who
> was superior.[44]

British diplomats took exception with the policy of kowtowing which led to increased tensions by the

mid-1800s. The situation came to a head over the trading of opium and challenged the centuries-old

status quo in China.

Opium Wars.

The Opium Wars were the pivotal point in Chinese history when the centuries-old, established

form of government came into conflict with a more scientifically and technologically advanced culture

from the West. By the end of the war, Great Britain had forced its way into China through treaty ports

which would ultimately lead to further imperialistic expansion. The established concept of the Mandate

from Heaven would also be questioned by the Chinese people.

In order to fully appreciate the significance of the Opium Wars, it is important to understand the

nature of China's trade with the outside world during the first half of the nineteenth century. Until this

time, the balance of trade with Europe heavily favored China.[45] This imbalance was further compounded

since the West did not have any commodity in significant quantity that China desired to purchase. British

---

[43] Ibid., 159.
[44] Ibid., 160.
[45] Pye, *China: An Introduction*, 101.

merchants introduced the sale of opium, in order to counter this imbalance and found a product that

ultimately resulted in a high demand by the Chinese people. Historian Jonathan Spence noted that,

> Massive British investments in the drug's manufacture and distribution, and the critical part that opium revenues played in Britain's' international balance-of-payments strategy, made the opium trade a central facet of that nation's foreign policy.[46]

In 1834, the British Parliament decided to end the monopoly the East India Company had over trade with

Asia. As a result, China was now open to trade with all nations, to include traders from across Europe

and the United States. As expected, opium sales to China increased. The Chinese imposed strict laws

against the buying and selling of opium, but the British traders found ways to bypass the regulations and

the Chinese demand for the addictive narcotic grew. To exacerbate the situation, Britain's first

superintendent for trade, Lord Napier, grew increasingly frustrated with having to trade through the

Cohong Merchants instead of being able to trade directly with Chinese government officials.[47] Tensions

came to a head in 1839 and war broke out.[48]

Over the course of the next three years, the Chinese suffered a series of military defeats and

ultimately signed a treaty favorable to Briton in order to prevent the British from attacking their capitol.

The Treaty of Nanjing was officially signed on 29 August 1842 aboard the *HMS Cornwallis*. Jeffry

Wasserstrom summarized the treaty in the following manner,

> As part of the Treaty of Nanjing signed at the conclusion of hostilities, Britain gained complete control over Hong Kong, which it held as a Crown colony until returning it to China in 1997. Britain also secured the right for its merchants and missionaries to set up self-governing settlements in several other cities, dubbed "treaty ports," including Shanghai; and the French and Americans, and later the Japanese, used force and threat of force to ensure that the same privileges were extended to their nationals.[49]

---

[46] Spence, *The Search for Modern China*, 139.

[47] Cohong Merchants were the designated representatives of the Chinese government to conduct the trade of opium with foreign powers.

[48] Jonathan Spence has cited four main reasons for the outbreak of war: the spread of opium addiction among the Chinese, foreign refusal to accept Chinese legal norms (kowtowing to the emperor and having to deal through the Cohong Merchants, changes in the international trade structure (opium sales were no longer a monopoly by the British East India Company), and the end of the West's intellectual admiration of China.

[49] Wasserstrom, *China in the 21ˢᵗ Century*, 28.

Historian Jonathan Spence noted this as, "the most important treaty settlement in China's modern history."[50]

The Opium Wars proved costly for China across all elements of national power and fundamentally changed the way China had dealt with foreign countries for centuries. Diplomatically, instead of China keeping the barbarians at bay and isolated to the furthest coastal reaches of the empire, the treaty ports became self contained foreign settlements that directly impacted China's economic life.[51] Historian John K. Fairbank noted,

> As applied in the treaty ports, extraterritoriality became a powerful tool for the opening of China because it made foreign merchants and missionaries, their goods and property, and to some extent their Chinese employees, converts, and hangers-on, all immune to Chinese authority.[52]

Since the treaty demanded that foreign powers be afforded the same privileges, the Chinese were unable to use their time-proven technique of playing barbarians against each other (through the careful management of favors granted to one barbarian that was unknown to another). China was also forced to establish a Foreign Office—a new concept which China did not need to bother with previously. Economically, China had to pay an indemnity of $21 million and suffered the loss of five port cities to foreign countries. Militarily, the Qing dynasty had been decisively defeated by a foreign force that was superior in both military innovations and tactics.[53] Lucian Pye noted, "The impact of the West was a completely different order, for it represented a political and military threat based on modern science and technology. China became aware they were facing a challenge unknown in their previous history." Perhaps most significantly the people began to question their historic ways and became anxious to prove themselves in this new modern world.[54] The concept of the Mandate from Heaven had been challenged by barbarians and lost. China's long standing superiority was now being fundamentally questioned. The Chinese interaction with the West in the nineteenth century was profoundly destabilizing. The impact of

---

[50] Spence, *The Search for Modern China*, 158. See Appendix for a listing of the twelve main articles of the Treaty of Nanjing.
[51] Pye, *China: An Introduction*, 113.
[52] Fairbank, *The United States and China*, 168.
[53] Spence, *The Search for Modern China*, 158.
[54] Pye, *China: An Introduction*, 117.

this is seen today by China's intense desire to ensure they are strong enough, both militarily and economically, to prevent a situation like this from happening again.

Taiping Uprising.

During the second half of the nineteenth century, China and the Qing dynasty continued to experience violence and civil unrest. The Taiping Uprising was one such insurrection that lasted from 1848-1864, resulting in the death of hundreds of thousands of Chinese. This uprising challenged the dynasty's authority and ability to maintain control over the population. It also was a harbinger of domestic frustration from which the seeds of revolution were beginning to take root.

The uprising was led by Hong Xiuquan who was frustrated with the Qing Dynasty's civil service examination policy. This exam policy was steeped in Confucian tradition and relied heavily on rote memorization of the Chinese classics. At the height of the insurrection, Hong controlled an area in China roughly the size of France. Hong's goal was to purge China from Manchu rule (Qing Dynasty) and establish a Christian state. Hong had delusional visions (hallucinations) that "convinced him he was Christ's younger brother and was destined to expel the Manchus."[55] Hong distorted Christianity to meet the rebellion's needs. He equated the Manchu dynasty with demons that were fighting against the one true God and as such the Manchu's "forces of Confucian belief swayed the Chinese away from the true path of righteousness."[56] Hong's bizarre form of Christianity alienated Western nations and caused them to side with the Qing Dynasty who eventually squelched the revolt.[57] Ultimately, the rebellion failed for a number of reasons: poor leadership (Hong became withdrawn and focused inwardly on sensual pleasures); the loss of several competent advisors; failure by Hong to establish any clear goals; failure to appeal to anti-Manchu establishment; failure to rally popular support from the peasants in the countryside

---

[55] Wasserstrom, *China in the 21ˢᵗ Century*, 29.
[56] Spence, *The Search for Modern China*, 172.
[57] Fairbank, *The United States and China*, 190. A small Sino-foreign mercenary force, called the 'Ever Victorious Army,' was led by an American (F.T. Ward) and the famous British commander (C. G. "Chinese" Gordon). It helped defeat the rebels around Shanghai.

21

(which meant they were not able to lead a social revolution in the villages); failure to coordinate with two other ongoing uprisings (the Nian Uprising in the north and the Red Turban Uprising in the south); and failure to obtain western support.[58] This uprising produced three significant results: the depletion of dynasty's finances after 14 years of prolonged fighting; the death of hundreds of thousands of Chinese; and the sullied reputation of Christianity which manifested itself again in the Boxer Rebellion.

First Sino-Japanese War.

China was not the only East Asian power to have to adapt itself to Europe and the United States in the latter nineteenth century. Japan had been forced to engage with the West after the United States employed gunboat diplomacy to open Japan. In the short term, Japan proved more adept than their Chinese neighbors at adapting to the Western imposed international system, so much so that by the end of the nineteenth century, Japan was increasingly asserting itself as the regional great power. In 1894, war broke out between Japan and China over the issue of who controlled Korea. China backed the Korean government and opposed Japanese forces attempting to occupy the peninsula. Although the Chinese ground forces were numerically superior to the Japanese, the Chinese were decisively defeated. At the same time, China's most modern force, the Chinese North Seas Fleet, was also attacked and lost several vessels which were either captured or sank. On 17 April 1895, the Chinese and Japanese signed the Treaty of Shimonoseki which effectively ended the war. Both countries ended up recognizing Korea as a separate nation, but China was forced to pay an indemnity to Japan of 200 million taels of silver (worth approximately $66 million). China also forfeited Formosa (modern day Taiwan), the Pescadore Islands, and agreed to lease the Liaotung Peninsula to Japan. The Chinese cities of Chungking, Soochow, and Hangchow were also forced open to commercial Japanese business.[59] This war marked another humiliating loss for China. Not only was further Chinese territory ceded to foreign powers, but it suffered

---

[58] Spence, *The Search for Modern China*, 173.

[59] Lawrence D. Higgins, "Modernization and Expansion of Japan," in *Brassey's Encyclopedia of Military History and Biography* (Washington: Brassey's Inc., 2000), 546.

22

the loss to a modernized Asian country that less than fifty years earlier had similarly been feudalistic in its ways of governing their country. The loss of 200 million taels of silver did not help the Qing dynasty's financial situation either. This war left a strong resentment between China and Japan which would be further exacerbated in the second Sino-Japanese War of 1937-1945. As Lucian Pye noted, "The fact that Japan felt no awe of the Celestial Kingdom and could handily defeat the Chinese was possibly the most demoralizing blow to China."[60] The Chinese distrust of the Japanese is still prevalent today and manifests itself with China's efforts to limit Japan's expansion, both economically and militarily, in the South China Sea.

Boxer Rebellion.

Japan's defeat of China set off a scramble by European powers, notably France, Germany, and Russia, to secure additional concessions for their own from the increasingly embattled Qing dynasty. This in turn led to an increased European presence that further incensed Chinese nationalists. The Boxer Rebellion was an uprising that was a direct result of continued imperialist expansion. By the end of the rebellion, the Manchu government proved unable to prevent foreign intervention and had lost control and legitimacy as a ruling body in China. The results of the rebellion set the conditions for the revolution that would occur a decade later.

The Boxer Rebellion lasted from 1899-1901 and was led by a "secret organization called the Society of the Righteous Harmonious Fists (thus Boxers)."[61] Both the Qing dynasty and their Chinese subjects were justifiably concerned about their country being carved up by foreign powers. The Boxer Rebellion was a manifestation of the Chinese nationalist response to (Japanese and) Western imperialism in China. Germany had used an attack on its missionaries to justify the occupation of the Shandong port city of Qingdao. The British forced the Chinese into a 99 year lease on a fertile farming area north of

---

[60] Pye, *China: An Introduction*, 115.
[61] Ernest R. and Trevor N. Dupuy, *Encyclopedia of Military History from 3500 B.C. to the Present* (New York: Harper and Rowe Publishers, 1977), 1008.

Hong Kong on the Kowloon peninsula. Russia had increased its presence in Manchuria and had occupied and fortified the city of Lushun. France claimed special rights in their Tonkin border provinces and on the island of Hainan. Japan continued to put pressure on Korea and intensified its economic efforts in China. Meanwhile, the United States declared an Open Door policy which stated that all countries would agree not to deny others access to their spheres of influence.[62] The Dowager Empress, Cixi, stated the following in her declaration of war:

> The foreigners have been aggressive towards us, infringed upon our territorial integrity, trampled our people under their feet…They oppress our people and blaspheme our gods. The common people suffer greatly at their hands, and each one of them is vengeful. Thus it is that the brave followers of the Boxers have been burning churches and killing Christians.[63]

Cixi, was a Qing (Manchu). By 1898 it was clear that Chinese nationalism was both increasingly anti-Western and Anti-Manchu. Deciding to side with the Boxers thus attempted to curry favor for the Qing dynasty (increasingly unpopular) by appearing anti-Western (which was popular). The Dowager Empress secretly used this proxy force of the Boxers to attack foreign missionaries and Chinese Christians. Violence spread when the Boxers began attacking symbols of imperial expansion such as railroads, telegraph lines, Western schools, and foreign diplomats. By the summer of 1900, foreign nations sent warships and troops to guard their legations at Beijing. Events came to a head on 20 June 1900 when a Chinese mob murdered the German Minister, Barron von Kettler, and besieged the foreign embassies at Beijing. The siege lasted until 14 August 1900 when an allied expeditionary force consisting of eight foreign nations (Austria-Hungary, Britain, France, Germany, Italy, Japan, Russia, and the United States) arrived and relieved the legations. From September 1900 until May 1901, the allied forces conducted a series of punitive missions in and around Beijing. On 12 September 1901, the Boxer Protocol was signed which officially ended the rebellion but again resulted in significant losses for the Qing Dynasty. Details of the Boxer Protocol included: the Chinese erecting monuments to the more than 200 Western dead; a moratorium of importing arms into China for two years; allowing permanent foreign guards to emplace

---

[62] Spence, *The Search for Modern China*, 231.
[63] Ibid., 233.

defensive weapons to protect the legation quarter in perpetuity; developing Zongli Yamen into a fully prestigious Ministry of Foreign Affairs; executing the leading Boxer supporters—to include the governor of Yuxian; and paying an indemnity of 450 taels, which was then worth about $333 million (this is significant considering the entire annual income for the Qing Dynasty was around 250 million taels).[64] Not only was suppression of the Boxer Rebellion a humiliating defeat by foreign powers, but it also imposed further unfair treaties and indemnities on China. This humiliation by foreign powers would repeat itself again following the Treaty of Versailles, which resulted in China losing several treaty ports. At the end of World War One, Germany's concessions in China were transferred to Japan rather than reverting to China. These events in the early part of the twentieth century left a lasting impression on China including a strong distrust of foreigners throughout the rest of the century.

Chinese Republic.

From 1905 until 1911, civil unrest continued in China. The assertion by the Chinese nationalists was that the old Confucian-based form of dynastic government was no longer suitable for the modern world. Foreign powers made increasing territorial demands on China and dissatisfaction with the Qing Dynasty continued. As a result of decades of war, the national finances were in ruin; the Chinese Army was unreliable, likely to mutiny, and hard to control; natural disasters devastated several harvests which, in turn, forced thousands of internal refugees; and foreign pressures against the Qing Dynasty continued.[65] Chinese nationalism continued to build along with revolutionary sentiments. Historians typically mark the beginning of the Chinese Revolution as 10 October 1911 when troops in Wuch'ang mutinied. The revolutionary goals were to establish a legitimate republic that would be able to discredit the ancient imperial form of government and transition China into a modern nation-state.[66] The marshal, Yuan Shih-k'ai, sent to quell the revolt, ironically ended up joining the movement in December. On 12 February

---

[64] Ibid., 235.
[65] Ibid., 271.
[66] Ibid.

25

1912 the child emperor, six-year-old Puyi, officially abdicated and the Chinese Republic was

established.[67] John Fairbank noted the significance of this event by stating:

> The end of the monarchy in 1912 marked the beginning of a prolonged crisis of authority and central power in the world's most ancient state...This abandonment of China's age-old focus of political life was possible because of nationalism had arisen to provide a new loyalty to the Chinese state, culture, and people. But this new nationalism had not yet found institutional expression.[68]

Sun Yat-sen, a medical student turned nationalist revolutionary, was elected as the republic's first

president. One of his major challenges was instituting the notion of a political party which was a foreign

concept considering the emperor had ruled for centuries through his bureaucracies. Sun became

disillusioned by the inefficiencies of a Western-style parliamentary system and as a result turned to

various warlords to achieve his revolutionary objectives.[69] Like other Chinese statesmen before him, he

saw a strong central state as essential to holding China together. However, within a year, Yuan overthrew

Sun.[70] Yuan had no faith in the Western liberal model and continued to strengthen his position as

president, basically turning it into a dictatorship. He purged all Guomingdang party members from

parliament and by 1914 had dissolved parliament completely.[71] For the next eight years, power struggles

continued over who would rule China. Yuan died in 1916 and was succeeded by Li Yuan-hung. The

northern military governors were displeased with Li's rule and revolted from May to August 1917. One

of the northern governors, Chang Hsun, briefly overthrew the Beijing government and re-established the

Manchu Dynasty. It lasted for a grand total of 12 days (1-12 July 1917). Ultimately, Li was overthrown

and Feng Kuo-chang assumed the presidency.[72] There are four primary reasons why the Revolution of

1911 failed: there was no common goal beyond overthrowing the Manchus; the general population was

not behind revolutionary movements; the Chinese still had a very strong fear of foreign intervention

---

[67] Dupuy, *Encyclopedia of Military History*, 1009.
[68] Fairbank, *The United States and China*, 220.
[69] Ibid., 225.
[70] Wasserstrom, *China in the 21st Century*, 37.
[71] Spence, *The Search for Modern China*, 283. Note: The Guomingdang was the Nationalist political party founded by Sun Yat-sen.
[72] Dupuy, *Encyclopedia of Military History*, 1010.

(reminiscent of the Boxer Rebellion); and the idea of a constitutional parliament could not be linked to any Chinese political tradition.[73]

4 May Movement.

When the peacemakers at Versailles awarded German concessions in China to Japan, it touched off a wide-spread protest movement. This movement is known as the 4 May Movement, after the date 4 May 1919, when the first protests against the territorial transfers took place in Beijing. The 4 May Movement resulted from increasing Chinese nationalism, continued distrust of foreign powers, and the continued search for a suitable form of government. On 4 May 1919, student protestors took to the streets of Beijing and demanded the return of Shangdon to Chinese control.[74] They protested the willingness of the warlord government to cede territory to foreign countries, especially Japan. They were also angered by the apparent governmental ambivalence regarding the sanctions that were to be imposed as a result of the Paris Peace Conference of World War I (Treaty of Versailles). These sanctions called for Germany's overseas possessions in China to be turned over to Japan instead of China. Despite the Chinese delegation's refusal to sign the Versailles Treaty, the sanctions took effect. The height of the unrest occurred in June when a general strike shut down the main commercial and financial sector in Shanghai.[75] The 4 May Movement marked a time of intense reflection for many of the educated Chinese. Historian Jonathan D. Spence described it as "a period of political insecurity and unparalleled intellectual self-scrutiny and exploration."[76] Concern spread about the future of China and whether or not it could maintain its autonomy. According to Spence, the educated elite began to "study every kind of political and organizational theory, examine the nature of their own social fabric, debate the values of new forms

---

[73] Fairbank, *The United States and China*, 223.

[74] The Five Resolutions of the 4 May Movement were: protest against the Shangdong settlement reached at the Versailles conference; student protestors sought to awaken 'the masses all over the country' to an awareness of China's plight; they proposed holding a mass meeting of the people in Peking; they urged the formation of a Peking student union; and they called for an immediate demonstration in protest of the Versailles treaty terms.

[75] Wasserstrom, *China in the 21ˢᵗ Century*, 39.

[76] Spence, *The Search for Modern China*, 271.

27

of education and language, and explore the possibilities for progress that seemed to lie at the heart of Western science."[77] The fall of the Qing dynasty created a vacuum that was not adequately filled by the Chinese Republic and its failed attempt to establish a parliamentary form of government. The failure of this type of government compelled some intellectual elite to look elsewhere. The Soviet Union, through the Communist International (COMINTERN) encouraged the development of the Chinese Communist Party.[78] The power vacuum was being filled by those who possessed raw physical power—the Chinese warlords.

Warlord Period.

As the fledgling Chinese republic grew weaker, the educated elite continued to search for a better form of government. The neighboring Soviet Union took advantage of the unrest and infiltrated several agents to further spread Marxist doctrine, which appealed to many as a possible way to counter the warlords, foreign intervention, and address the grievances of Chinese workers.[79] By 1921, the Chinese Communist Party (CCP) was holding regular meetings which enabled the party to establish itself in China. From 1920-1926, the government's rule over much of China weakened to a point that allowed numerous warlords to seize power, hence giving the name to this period in China's tumultuous history. In 1923, Sun Yat-sen, as leader of the Guomindang, went to drastic efforts to unite China and fight the warlords. He accepted help from the Soviet Union and united the Guomindang with the Chinese Communist Party.[80] For the next three years, the Guomindang and the CCP worked together to rid China of the warlords. They initially gained control in southern China and spread their efforts northward. In 1925, Sun Yat-sen died and leadership of the Guomindang transferred to Chiang Kai-shek. By 1926, the unified efforts of the Guomindang and the CCP were having considerable military successes. In 1926,

---

[77] Ibid.

[78] Note: The COMINTERN was a subversive organization of the Soviet Union that was dedicated to the spread of communism throughout the world.

[79] Spence, *The Search for Modern China*, 272.

[80] Ibid., 805.

Chiang launched a two year military campaign, called the Northern Expedition, to eradicate the remaining warlord control and unify China under one government.[81] In July of 1927, Chiang became aware of a communist plot to take control of the government and began a purge of all communists from government positions. He also expelled all Soviet advisors. On 1 August 1927, an uprising occurred at Nanchang between communist and Nationalist forces which marked the beginning of the 22-year Chinese Civil War. Although the insurrection was put down, 1 August is celebrated by the communists as the birth of the People's Liberation Army (PLA). The insurrection was suppressed by loyal government troops who pursued the communist rebels all the way to the south China coast. A small remnant of communists, led by Chu Te, escaped to the mountainous region of western Kiangsi.[82] The Warlord Period proved that China would have to be united through force. Between the 1911 Revolution and the Communist Party's conquest of the mainland in 1949, the future of China remained highly contested. The stage was now set for civil war.

Chinese Civil War.

The Chinese Civil War was fought from 1927 until 1949 between Nationalist and communist forces. During the war, Mao Zedong would emerge as the leader of the Chinese Communist Party and the Nationalists would conduct a ruthless campaign to purge the communists from China. In the end, it would be Chiang's inability to effectively rule the government and rally support from the population that would enable a communist victory.

It was in the western region of China where Mao Zedong, a leader in the CCP's politburo, started to emerge as the predominant leader of the communist forces. On 9 September 1927, Mao directed another uprising, called "Autumn Harvest," against the Nationalist forces of Chiang Kai-shek and his

---

[81] Ibid., 801.
[82] Dupuy, *Encyclopedia of Military History*, 1044.

Guomindang Party. Although it failed, Soviet leader Joseph Stalin directed a third communist uprising in December of that year in Canton. After four days of fighting, this uprising was also suppressed.[83]

From 1928-1931, Chiang consolidated his Nationalist gains in eastern and southern China, defeating controlling warlords and purging the communists from the urban areas. Mao and his communist forces reverted to guerrilla tactics and took sanctuary in the Chingkang Mountains. In 1930, the Nationalist forces launched a series of "bandit extermination" campaigns designed to further purge the communists from areas they still held. Mao had control of a region near Juichin with a population of 50 million. On 15 October 1934, Mao and his communist forces, consisting of approximately 100,000 men, began their 6000 mile trek known as the "Long March."[84] During the Long March, Mao consolidated his power as the head of the CCP, ensuring his supporters remained in key leadership positions. He also studied and improved his theory on guerrilla warfare. The Chinese Civil War continued, but in 1937, the Nationalist and CCP forces declared a suspension of hostilities in order to present a united front against the impending attack from Japanese forces.

On 7 July 1937, the Japanese declared war against China and began successfully capturing eastern and central China. By 28 July, the Japanese had captured Beijing, and Tientsin fell on 29 July. Shanghai was seized on 8 November and the Chinese Nationalist capital, Nanking, fell on 13 December after a three month siege. 1937 marked the beginning of the Second Sino-Japanese War for China, which later merged into World War Two. The war devastated China, further weakening Chiang's overall control of the country. Inflation spiraled out of control and prices increased by 2500 percent.[85] The Guomindang was also plagued with corruption and inefficiencies, which would later prove part of their downfall. Chiang and the Nationalist forces were forced to relocate their government from Nanking to Chungking in the western province of Szechuan in order to survive. Although the communist and

---

[83] David Rees, "Red Star in the East," in *War in Peace, Conventional and Guerrilla Warfare Since 1945*, ed. Robert Thompson (New York: Harmony Books, 1981), 2.
[84] Ibid.
[85] Ibid., 3.

Nationalist forces were technically at a truce, Mao took advantage of this tumultuous period to infiltrate forces back into eastern and central China.

Following World War Two, hostilities resumed between the communist and Nationalist forces. The civil war intensified from 1945 to 1949, with each side receiving external support. Chiang and the Nationalists received aid from the United States; Mao and the CCP received support from the Soviet Union. In 1945, the United States sent General George C. Marshall to assess the situation in China. He attempted to establish two truces between the warring factions, but neither lasted long. In 1946, the Nationalist forces outnumbered the communist forces three to one. However, the communists continued to retain their control over the rural areas in northern China and Manchuria. The PLA launched their Manchurian Offensive in September 1948 and successfully captured Changchun and Mukden. Even though the United States had supported Chiang and the Nationalists since World War Two, it was at this point when President Truman decided that no American forces would be used to support the Nationalists. The final campaign was launched by the CCP in November of 1948. It resulted in the capture of a critical railway junction in vicinity of Hsuchow in northern China on 10 January 1949. Communist forces entered Beijing on 21 January 1949 and Mao declared the establishment of the People's Republic of China (PRC) on 1 October 1949, basically ending the Chinese Civil War. Chiang and his Nationalist government were forced to retreat to the island of Formosa (Taiwan) where they established Taipei as their capital. Taiwan remains independent from communist China to this day.[86]

Mao Zedong was able to win the Chinese Civil War by not only persevering under unusual hardships but also by his rallying of the popular support of the population. During the long struggle, Mao learned how to adapt his fighting methods to fit the situation and developed his theory of guerrilla warfare. Ultimately, he succeeded in unifying China for the first time in over 100 years which marked the beginning of the end of China's Century of Humiliation.

---

[86] Ibid.

There are three observations and two behavioral characteristics that can be derived from this review of Chinese history. The first observation is that the Opium Wars, the First Sino-Japanese War, and the Boxer Rebellion all resulted in humiliating defeats by foreign powers which led intensified the distrust between China and foreigners. The second observation is that the Taiping Uprising, the Warlord Period, and the Chinese Civil War ravaged the country side, killed thousands of Chinese, and left the country extremely war weary. The third observation is that the attempt to establish a Republic and the 4 May Movement demonstrated China's acknowledgement that the historic methods of Chinese government, which had worked for centuries, were no longer a suitable form of government for the industrialized world of the twentieth century. The two behavioral characteristics that reveal themselves in the form of nationalistic desires are: China's intense desire to have a military that is strong enough to secure and defend its territorial boundaries; and China's desire to regain the great power status it once had along with international respect that goes with this status.

Summary.

From this brief review of influential Chinese philosophies, strategic concepts, and modern Chinese history, a construct can be developed through which one may view enduring strategic principles. This strategic lens includes three principles with corresponding methods to achieve the desired end state. The enduring principles are: the indirect approach, timing (to include persistence, patience, and setting the conditions for victory), and adaptability (realizing conditions are constantly in a state of change). Both Chinese history and philosophical concepts are replete with examples of each of these enduring strategic principles, illustrated in the following table:

Chinese Strategic Lens	
Principle	**Method**
Indirect Approach	- Avoid the enemy's strength - Orthodox vs. Unorthodox - Attack the enemy's weak points and vulnerabilities
Timing: Persistence, Patience, and setting the Conditions for Victory	- Allow events to unfold - Develop an imbalance that can be exploited (often through deception) - Have a deliberate plan - Only strike when conditions are right
Adaptability: Realize conditions are constantly in flux	- Know your desired end state - Know your own gaps and the capacity you need to develop

Figure 1 Enduring Strategic Principles.

Mao Zedong's development of his theory on guerrilla warfare, during World War Two and the Chinese Civil War, is a classic example of all three principles rolled into one. Mao knew in both cases his communist forces were not strong enough to attack the Japanese and Nationalists directly, so he relied on the indirect approach. Mao played to his strengths and used hit and run tactics denying the enemy the ability to mass their forces against his smaller guerrilla forces. In addition, he withdrew his forces into the countryside rather than focusing on the large population centers and cities which were traditionally considered more valuable terrain to control. Attacking enemy vulnerabilities, such as extended supply lines, also demonstrated use of the indirect approach. Regarding the principle of time, Mao remained persistent in his struggle to achieve his desired end state. His famous Long March is espoused as a classic example of endurance and sacrifice for the greater good and ultimate cause. Mao's guerrilla tactics also focused on setting the conditions for victory before attacking. If the conditions were not right, he simply would not attack. Regarding adaptability, Mao knew that he eventually would need conventional forces,

33

not just guerrillas, to defeat the Nationalists. He accepted military supplies from the Soviet Union and carefully bided his time until he could build up forces strong enough to engage and defeat the Nationalists.

The principle of timing is apparent in both Daoist thinking and Chinese strategic concepts. The Daoist notion of *wu-wei* is described as going with the flow and letting the situation develop. Sun Tzu's examples of using deception and creating an imbalance also reflect an understanding of the principle of timing, which stresses patience by setting the conditions for victory before one acts. The ancient board game *GO* also reflects this timing principle of since one must patiently allow the situation to develop in order to adapt and win.

Regarding adaptability, Chinese history provides excellent examples of how this principle has been applied. In 1923, Sun Yat-sen accepted help from ideological opponents, the Soviet Union and the Chinese Communist Party (CCP), in order to gain the military and financial support required to defeat the Chinese warlords who still controlled much of China's provinces. Another example is the truce between the Guomingdang and the CCP, during World War Two, in order to unite efforts and drive the Japanese out of mainland China. The Daoist concept of *yin-yang* demonstrates an understanding that things are in a constant state of change. The dragon analogy is an excellent example of this notion of constant evolution and how one must remain flexible and adapt to the situation. Sun Tzu summed up the notion of adaptability as well in his axiom of knowing yourself and knowing the enemy. The intent of this concept is to gain situational understanding so one might know how to adapt before the conditions are right for victory.

China's Stated Core Interests and Means to Achieve Their Goals.

This monograph has examined recent Chinese history and philosophy to provide insights into Chinese strategic thought. With this foundation established, it is now appropriate to continue the examination of China from 1949 (the establishment of the People's Republic of China) to the present. A review of China's desired international status, the political challenges their leadership has struggled with, and China's efforts to modernize its military illustrate the complexities the PRC has had to deal with as they strive to put their past behind them and restore their status as a regional power.

As the preceding narrative suggests, Chinese statesmen are concerned with maintaining both internal harmony and security in the international system. Any Chinese statesman reflecting on the widespread perception of the Century of Humiliation could be expected to emphasize the need for internal unity and external strength to prevent any repetition from past frustrations. Two major lessons from studying modern Chinese history is their justifiable extreme distrust of foreign intervention and a burning desire for recognition as a regional power—an acknowledgement of their rightful place in Asia, if not the globe. The Chinese consider the hundred years before the rise of the CCP as the "Century of Humiliation,"[87] and as such, each leader of the People's Republic of China, from Chairman Mao to the current president Hu Jintao, has charted a path to restore China to its rightful place in Asia. The key milestones along this path to power are gaining international respect and becoming a major economic player. As China struggled to establish a modernized industrial base, it first sought to gain a modicum of international respect through the use of military force.

In 1950, Mao Zedong justified Chinese intervention in the Korean War based on security concerns. His general, Peng Dehuai, summed the concerns in the following manner:

> If we allow the enemy (the United States) to occupy the entire Korean peninsula, the threat to our country is very great. In the past when the Japanese invaded China they used Korea as a springboard. First they attacked our three eastern provinces, then using these as a springboard; they launched a large scale offensive against the interior. We cannot overlook this lesson of history. We must fight the enemy now, we cannot hesitate.[88]

Mao also hoped to gain the respect of the international community by demonstrating a willingness to stand up a coalition led by the most powerful nation on the earth.

The issue of respect also revealed itself on two other occasions: the 1962 border war with India and the 1979 border war with Vietnam. In both cases, China exercised the use of force justified on a

---

[87] Li Jijun, *Traditional Military Thinking and the Defensive Strategy of China* (Carlisle Barracks: Strategic Studies Institute, August 1997), 2.

[88] Kenneth D. Johnson, *China's Strategic Culture: A Perspective for the United States* (Carlisle Barracks: Strategic Studies Institute, June 2009), 18.

perceived arrogance of the two countries as well as means to resolve the boundary dispute.[89] According

to historian William H. Mott IV, China used both of these conflicts to not only punish what he calls the so

called "arrogant" country, but to also teach a lesson to neighboring countries to not interfere in Chinese

affairs and remind the attacked country of their proper places in China's perceived world.[90] While these

military actions may not have achieved the global international respect China sought, these conflicts did

buy time for the CCP as it focused on internal and economic reforms.

China's Political Challenge.

China's modernization efforts have not been easy. A review of China's political leadership

reveals the complexity the PRC has struggled with along its path of gaining international recognition as a

respected Asian power. The repeating pattern is one of the leader rising to power, his struggle to

consolidate and maintain control, and his ultimate transition based on either his death or the Party's

influence.

Mao Zedong ruled as General Secretary of the Chinese Communist Party from 1949 until his

death in 1976. Under his leadership, he was able to establish strong centralized control and authority in

China. With the help of the Soviet Union, Mao sought to develop China's industrial base, while the state

owned the major means of production and collectively owned the means of agriculture. By enforcing

Leninist policies, Mao ensured social economic organizations were suppressed. Mao remained in power

and continued to strengthen his position. He developed a cult of personality through skilful manipulation

of his political opponents and dealt with his enemies ruthlessly. In the end, Mao succeeded in established

a very strong communist party, centralized government and army. While he was able to put a strong

group of revolutionary followers in power, he later set them against each other. By manipulating others,

he forced people and organizations to rely on him to resolve conflicts and remain dependent on him

---

[89] William H. Mott IV and Jae Chang Kim, *The Philosophy of Chinese Military Culture* (New York: Palgrave MacMillan, 2006), 225.
[90] Ibid., 227.

36

exclusively. Political science professor, Kenneth Lieberthal described this in the following manner, "Mao utilized rectification campaigns and other methods to prevent power centers from developing. In the system he sought to create, administration would be decentralized and flexible, while power would be highly centralized under his personal control."[91] Mao's methods worked, while he was alive, but left the country in turmoil upon his death.

Deng Xiaoping followed Mao in 1976 and as journalist Richard McGregor describes, "Deng Xiaoping threw out Mao's destructive notions and returned the party organization to its Leninist roots, as an empowered elite providing enlightened leadership to the masses."[92] Deng espoused that, "China should observe calmly; secure position; cope with affairs calmly; hide our capabilities and bide our time; be good at maintaining a low profile; and never claim leadership."[93] This dictum served China well and allowed the nation to focus on improving conditions internally while still maintaining a degree of contact with the outside world. Deng is responsible for reassessing Mao's programs and allowing China to make necessary economic reforms. By opening up to the rest of the world, Deng was able to obtain the much needed capital, technology, and intellectual knowledge needed to develop his country economically. One of Deng's most significant breakthroughs was in achieving official recognition of the PRC by the United States as the official government of China.

Ultimately, Deng refused to give up power and considered himself, just like his predecessor Mao, indispensible. Deng purged those he previously designated as his successor. His administration was also plagued by corruption among the leading institutions. Under Deng's regime, the "Politburo became a committee of protégés who answered to the real power behind the scenes, the elderly patrons whose deals

---

[91] Kenneth Lieberthal, *Governing China: From Revolution to Reform, Second Edition.* (New York: W. W. Norton and Company), 121.
[92] Richard McGregor, *The Party: The Secret World of China's Communist Rulers* (New York: Harper Collins Publishers, 2010), 14.
[93] DOD, *Annual Report to Congress,* 27.

among themselves determined who would serve on the party's top bodies."[94] Deng remained in power until 1987, when he was demoted by the CCP for taking too soft of a stance against student protests.[95]

Zhao Ziyang followed Deng and implemented several important economic reforms. Ironically, the same fate followed Zhao for taking too soft a stance against the Tiananmen Uprising protestors and he was replaced by Jiang Zemin in 1989. Jiang rose to power following the crisis, but was very careful to court the good graces of Deng who remained in control behind the scenes. Jiang did not fully take charge until Deng's death in 1997, but continued to make major economic reforms in China. For the next eight years, Jiang continued to build up his power base, establish his own control, and remove rivals until Deng's death. Part of Jiang's success was due to the fact that Deng was growing progressively weaker in health and was too weak to organize a move to replace him.

Hu Jintao's rise to power was characterized by patience and setting the conditions for success. For example, in 1993 Hu became the head of the Central Party School. The Central Party School is the institution of higher education that trains selected individuals for leadership positions within the Chinese Communist Party. From this position as head of the Central Party School, Hu could affect the future of the Party. He continued to handle matters very deftly, being careful to avoid creating enemies. Over time he built his reputation as a hard working consensus building and was chosen to succeed Jiang in 2002. As Kenneth Lieberthal has described, Hu Jintao "followed a very patient strategy to ascend to the top party post...He built up a reputation for being very smart, effective, disciplined, modest, and loyal."[96] Hu remains in power as of the writing of this manuscript. Under his watch, China has done much to regain international stature. China has secured membership in the International Monetary Fund and also hosted the 2008 Olympics. More importantly, China has also clearly emerged as a key player on the global market. In 2007, Shanghai surpassed Hong Kong as the world's largest port based on the volume of

---

[94] Lieberthal, *Governing China*, 153.
[95] Wasserstrom, *China in the 21st Century*, 69.
[96] Lieberthal, *Governing China*, 155.

cargo handled,[97] and in 2010, China had a GDP growth of 8.2% compared to the United State's GDP growth of only 1.3%.[98] These events are important steps for China as it overcomes their 'Century of Humiliation' and regains its international stature. The question, however, is how will China interact both regionally in Asia and globally. Will they remain content as a regional power, or will they seek to displace the United States in its role as the dominant power in the Pacific?

A Harmonious World.

In 2004, Hu proposed the idea of a 'harmonious world' in order to further portray the image of a peacefully, yet rapidly developing nation.[99] The use of this rhetoric also provides a way for the Party to abandon the (now) less useful tenets of Marxist-Leninism and provides a tool for Chinese soft power like their establishment of Confucian institutions around the world. According to Georgetown Professor Robert G. Sutter, this 'harmonious world' approach was based on:

> Careful consideration of China's modernization experience of the past twenty-five years, and represented an effort to set forth a vision of China's future development that would be compatible with China's interests and those of its neighbors and concerned powers, notably the United States.[100]

Sutter describes China taking a more 'pragmatic' approach as they integrate into the global system while recognizing the dominance of the United States. Since the early 1990s, in line with Deng's dictum, China has coped with international affairs while quietly biding its time. They have even gone to the point of letting the United States take the lead on several issues of mutual interest such as securing the sea lines of communication, keeping stability on the Korean peninsula, and providing leadership on the war on terrorism. However, it is important to note that China has stressed the importance of developing on "the basis of its own resources and abilities without seeking control of others or expansion." [101] To this extent, in December 2010 Chinese State Councilor, Dai Bingguo, listed China's core interests as:

---

[97] Kaplan, *Monsoon*, 282.
[98] Daniel Franklin, ed. "The World in 2012," in *The Economist* (January 2012), 115.
[99] Baogang Gao and Sujian Gao, "Thirty Years of China-U.S. Relations: Reappraisals and Reassessment" in *Thirty Years of China-U.S. Relations* (Plymouth, UK: Lexington Books, 2010), 5.
[100] Sutter, *China's Rise in Asia*, 266.
[101] Ibid., 267.

The state system, political system, and political stability of China; that is the leadership of the CCP, the socialist system, and the path of socialism with Chinese characteristics.

The sovereignty and security, territorial integrity, and national unity of China.

The basic guarantee for the sustained development of the economy and society of China. [102]

Keeping the CCP in power, maintaining China's sovereignty, and sustaining the current levels of economic and social development are recurring themes that aim at the heart of the CCP's political elite's decision making. As mentioned earlier, both Deng Xiaoping and his successor, Zhao Ziyang, were criticized and ultimately marginalized by the CCP for not taking a hard enough stance against protestors who were seen as a threat to the Party's control. Maintaining sovereignty and security, territorial integrity, and national unity of China have also been used by the CCP to justify the buildup of military forces, the People's Liberation Army (PLA). However, this would not be possible without a successful Chinese economy. In order to sustain China's growing economy, it desperately needs resources, particularly energy resources, which leads to an area of potential future confrontation—the South China Sea.

In his 2010 book, *Monsoon*, Robert D. Kaplan discusses how the Indian Ocean is becoming the new geostrategic location for this new century. He states, "the Indian Ocean will be where global power dynamics will be revealed…it constitutes the new Great Game in geopolitics." [103] The ability for a nation to sustain development and secure the resources needed for this development is what is driving this Great Game. Kaplan goes on to discuss the rising demand for energy requirements from both India and China and how it is estimated that the current demands will increase by 50 percent—and almost half of this will be by China and India alone. In a recent report to Congress, the Department of Defense stated that, "in 2009, China imported approximately 56 percent of its oil and conservative estimates project that China will import almost two thirds of its oil by 2015 and three quarters by 2030."[104] However, the challenge for China is the location of these energy resources—primarily the Middle East, Africa, Central Asia, and

---

[102] DOD, *Annual Report to Congress*, 23.
[103] Kaplan, *Monsoon*, 13.
[104] DOD, *Annual Report to Congress*, 30.

possibly the South China Sea. Since China is positioned east of these primary resource locations, the majority of any oil or natural gas that is extracted has to flow to China via the sea lanes (or Sea Lines of Communication—SLOC), with the exception of Central Asia. Because of this, China is extremely dependent on commercial shipping which must transit through the southwest Pacific to reach home ports in China, the strategic choke point being the Strait of Malacca. As of 2011, it was reported that over 83 percent of China's energy requirements pass through this location.[105] While there are proposed gas and oil pipelines to be constructed through central Asia, the overwhelming majority of energy resources still travel to China via the sea. This heavy dependence on the SLOCs has driven China's energy strategy to gain access to modern deepwater ports. China has gone out of its way to invest heavily, both diplomatically and economically, in friendly countries along the southern coastlines of Europe and Asia. Kaplan states, "A new and more complex order is gradually emerging in the maritime rimland of Eurasia, which includes not only the Indian Ocean but the western Pacific."[106] Kaplan claims that "China's demand for energy motivates both its foreign policy and national security policy."[107] The 2011 Department of Defense report to Congress corroborates this by stating, China, "motivated by expanding economic and security interests...is now venturing into the global maritime domain, a sphere long dominated by the U.S. Navy."[108] This expansion of both economic and security interests bring into question whether or not the idea of a 'harmonious world' can actually be attained.

---

[105] Ibid.
[106] Kaplan, *Monsoon*, 277.
[107] Ibid., 282.
[108] DOD, *Annual Report to Congress*, 11.

41

Since beginning its reforms in 1978, China has made a concerted effort in three areas: strengthening its economy, modernizing its military, and enabling the CCP to maintain power. China watchers have noted that China has taken a pragmatic approach to achieve these goals and has deliberately taken a long-term approach to achieving great power status. China sees the twenty-first century as a "strategic window of opportunity" and as such, has deliberately chosen to avoid a confrontation with the United States. They see, "stable relations with the U.S. and China's neighbors as

_____

essential to stability and critical to maximizing this window of opportunity."[110] However, of concern to the United States is the fact that China's defense budget, over the last 20 years, has steadily increased and is expected to rise by 8 to 10 percent annually in the next few years.[111] In December 2010, Defense Minister Liang Guanglie stated that two major cornerstones for rejuvenating China are "making the country prosperous and making the armed forces strong."[112] The Department of Defense has noted that, "China's leaders routinely emphasize the goal of reaching critical economic and military benchmarks by 2020 and eventually becoming a world-class economic and military power by 2050."[113] A review of China's military modernization efforts reveals that while their rhetoric may speak of a 'harmonious world,' their actions reflect a growing capability that some are concerned may challenge the current status quo in the Pacific.

Military Modernization.

In order to fully appreciate the PLA's modernization efforts, it is useful to understand its relationship with the CCP and formative events that has affected the PLA's decision making over the last 20 years. Mao Zedong noted that "Political power grows out the barrel of a gun!" But he also warned that, "our principle is that the party commands the gun, and the gun must never be allowed to command the party."[114] This very succinctly describes the current tension that exists between the People's Liberation Army and the Chinese Communist Party. The party wants more control over the military and the military wants more autonomy. This is the case in China. While the military's desire for more autonomy may seem like a natural evolution of a profession of arms, this presents a dilemma for China. Professor of political science, David Shambaugh, has noted:

---

[110] Ibid., 23.
[111] Kaplan, *Monsoon*, 282.
[112] DOD, *Annual Report to Congress*, 19.
[113] Ibid., 23.
[114] Shambaugh, *Modernizing China's Military*, 16.

43

In political systems dominated by a communist party, the PRC included, the military is an instrument of the party. It brings the party to power in violent revolution and uses occasional coercion and force to keep it in power. Its national security mission is a dual one targeting both internal and external enemies.[115]

When the military was called upon to suppress the 1989 Tiananmen Square uprising, it was considered normal and legitimate.[116] However, as Shambaugh has opined that many of the "many of the senior commanders were resentful of the renewed emphasis on politicization in the wake of 4 June (1989)—and many were perhaps privately opposed to the use of the military for domestic security purposes."[117] This reflects a possible tension that exists internally between the PLA and the CCP.

There is also an ongoing struggle between the hard liners and soft liners in the PRC. Hardliners espouse a more defiant role, where as soft liners recommend remaining engaged with foreign powers on contentious issues and prefer negotiations.[118] While there is occasional saber rattling, and papers have been published by senior ranking military officials with titles such as "Unrestricted Warfare," Political scientist, Professor June T. Dreyer, noted in her paper, *China's Strategic View*, "there is no conclusive evidence to support the assumption that what advice the PLA gives favors an assertive strategic stance. Most officers are patriotic…but they are also acutely aware of the PLA's military deficiencies."[119] These deficiencies were made apparent after China witnessing the coalition's rapid victory over Iraqi forces in Operation Desert Storm in 1991, and were again reinforced during the Taiwan Crisis of 1996. These led to an all out effort by China to modernize its military. According to Dreyer's study, in 1996 the "PLA was not considered a 'potent fighting force' and were 10-20 years behind the state of the art."[120] This is no longer the case with China's military. They have made major advancements in modernization and have even launched their first aircraft carrier this past year.

There are four areas of concern regarding the modernization of China's military: ballistic missiles, the PLA's navy, ground forces, and Space/Cyber capabilities. China's near-term objective

---

[115] Ibid., 12.
[116] Ibid., 16.
[117] Ibid., 29.
[118] Dreyer, *China's Strategic View*, 2.
[119] Ibid., 6.
[120] Ibid.

continues to be preparing military forces for 'Taiwan Strait contingencies.' This is evident from the fact that several of China's most modern weapon systems are being positioned in the military regions nearest to the island of Taiwan. In the 2011 Department of Defense report to Congress, the department noted that:

> China's long-term, comprehensive military modernization is improving the PLA's capacity to conduct high-intensity, regional military operations, including —anti-access and area denial (A2AD) operations. The terms —anti-access and area denial, refer to capabilities that could be employed to deter or counter adversary forces from deploying to, or operating within, a defined space.[121]

Recently, China has made modernizing and developing land-based ballistic and cruise missiles a priority. They continue to acquire increasing numbers of very accurate cruise missiles that have a range exceeding 185 kilometers. China is able to produce the DH-10 land attack cruise missile (LACM), the ground and ship-launched YJ-62 anti-ship cruise missile (ASCM), and continues to acquire Russian-made ASCM's and fit them on their KILO-class diesel-electric attack submarines. It was reported that by December of 2010, China had deployed up to 1200 short range ballistic missiles (SRBM) to the military regions directly opposite Taiwan. China is also developing an anti-ship ballistic missile (ASBM), called the DF-21D, which has a range greater than 1500 kilometers and can be armed with a maneuverable warhead. The DF-21D would enable China to attack large ships, such as aircraft carriers, in the western Pacific.[122]

The Chinese navy, commonly referred to as the PLA Navy, consists of 75 principle surface ships, at least 60 submarines, 55 amphibious ships, and approximately 85 missile equipped small combatants, such as the new HOUBEL-class (Type 022) wave-piercing, catamaran hull, missile patrol boats. In 2011, the PLA Navy launched their first aircraft carrier—a rebuilt Soviet-era carrier called the *Varyag*. It is believed that China has the capacity to construct its own indigenous carrier, with the ability to build several carriers and necessary support ships, over the next ten years. Of great concern is the development

---

[121] DOD, *Annual Report to Congress*, 12.
[122] Ibid., 13.

of the PLA Navy's submarine fleet, the primary workhorse being the 13 modern, diesel-powered attack submarines of the SONG-class (type 039).[123]

China's air force currently consists of approximately 490 aircraft, all of which have the range to reach Taiwan without refueling. While several of these aircraft are considered fourth generation, their sheer numbers and ability to range Taiwan still present a credible force.[124] The PLA continues to acquire more advanced aircraft and has made a concerted effort to modernize its air defense batteries by purchasing several Russian exported SA-20 (PMU2) surface to air missiles.[125]

The size of the PLA's ground forces is estimated to be approximately 1.25 million Soldiers. 40,000 of these troops are located in the military regions directly opposite Taiwan. The PLA continues to modernize its ground forces with priority going to the units potentially designated for any Taiwan contingency. This modernization includes upgrading their main battle tank to a third-generation variant called the Type-99, developing new amphibious assault vehicles, and developing new multiple launch rocket systems.[126]

Advances in China's space and cyberwarfare capabilities continue as well. In 2010, China conducted 15 space launches, several of which had payloads capable of carrying satellites for communication, surveillance, navigation and meteorological purposes. 2010 also saw a number of computer systems around the world, including the United States government, targeted for intrusion to extract information. The origin of these intrusions appears to have been within China. These intrusions are of concern since they demonstrate the skills and access required to conduct computer network attacks (CNA).[127]

---

[123] Ibid., 14.

[124] Fourth Generation aircraft are those fielded between 1980-2010. Examples are multi-role fighters such as the French Mirage 2000 or the Lockheed Martin F-16. These are in contrast to Fifth Generation aircraft such as the F-117 and B2 which use stealth technology to reduce their signature and avoid detection.

[125] DOD, *Annual Report to Congress*, 14.

[126] Ibid., 15.

[127] Ibid.

This review of China's current military capability clearly shows that China is well on its way to having a modernized and internationally respected military. Of alarm is the amount of money China continues to invest in its defense which begs the question: what are China's ultimate intentions and how much military capability is enough?

Military Strategy.

China espouses a military strategy called the Active Defense. The PLA has stated the following as their tenets of Active Defense:

> —Overall, our military strategy is defensive. We attack only after being attacked. But our operations are offensive.
>
> —Space or time will not limit our counter-offensive.
>
> —We will not put boundaries on the limits of our offenses.
>
> —We will wait for the time and conditions that favor our forces when we do initiate offensive operations.
>
> —We will focus on the opposing force's weaknesses. [129]

The 2011Defense Report to Congress states it is apparent that China continually reviews and assesses its military strategy based on the ever changing nature of modern warfare. The 1989 collapse of the Soviet Union and the 1991 Persian Gulf War clearly had an impact on their strategy.[130] The recent emphasis on expanding their naval capabilities also indicates a condition in China that hasn't existed for centuries—no perceived threat along China's borders. China has also dedicated a concerning amount of time to asymmetric and network-centric warfare, as well as anti-access/area denial (A2AD) capabilities, over the past decade which might possibly enable China the ability to deny "elements of the modern battle space to potential enemies." China's 2008 Defense White Paper stated their "guidelines emphasize fighting and winning local wars under conditions of informatization and building toward integrated joint operations, with a stress on asymmetric warfare to —make the best use of our strong points to attack the enemy's weak points."[131]

Analyzing China's military strategy through the lens of the enduring strategic principles is revealing. First, they deliberately state that their intentions are defensive. This indicates an effort to not deliberately portray a hostile or offensive nature which might incur unwanted diplomatic sanctions

---

[129] Ibid., 32.
[130] Ibid.
[131] Ibid.

48

against China or military operations by other nations in areas deemed sensitive to China's territory. China is sensitive to what has been referred to as the "China Threat" theory and considers this, "a serious hazard to the country's international standing and reputation, threatening the development of a persistent alignment of regional and global powers in opposition to China."[132] Secondly, the Chinese publicly state that they will deliberately wait and not strike until the conditions are correct, or favorable, for their success. This indicates a more patient and deliberate approach that allows events to unfold in order to possibly create an imbalance that could later be exploited. This illustrates the enduring strategic principles of timing, especially regarding patience and setting the conditions for victory—reminiscent of Sun Tzu. Third, they clearly state their desire to use the indirect approach where they will focus on the enemy's weakness. By doing this, they can avoid the enemy's strength and exploit his vulnerabilities. Hence, there is an emphasis on asymmetric and cyberwarfare. Lastly, by reviewing and constantly assessing their military strategy, the Chinese demonstrate the principle of adaptability. They realize that conditions are ever changing on the modern battlefield and one must look for gaps and capabilities that need to be developed in order to achieve victory.

There is one important dynamic that needs to be highlighted when discussing Chinese military strategy and that is the tension between the Chinese tradition of secrecy and deception vice a growing and obvious military capability. As China continues to develop and test more modern military equipment and capabilities, such as aircraft carriers and ballistic missiles, their ability to conceal these advances will be more and more difficult, if not impossible, to hide. These modernizing military capabilities, in light of the theory that communist China is or remains a threat, demonstrate an obvious contradiction to the proposed peaceful rise of China and what President Hu espouses as "harmonious world." This contradiction is most obvious when examining the case of Taiwan.

---

[132] Ibid., 36.

Taiwan.

At the end of the Chinese Civil War in 1949, Chiang Kai-shek and his Nationalist government fled mainland China to the island of Formosa (current day Taiwan) and established their government's capital at Taiping. In support of this democratic government and in direct opposition to Mao's PRC, the United States refused to recognize the communist government in Beijing and instead recognized Taiping as the official government of China. This ended in 1979 when the United States decided to reverse its official position and recognized the PRC. Even with official recognition by the United States, the PRC declared it would still seek to unify China by obtaining Taiwan, through peaceful means if possible, but military means if necessary. In a response to this, on 10 April 1979, the United States Congress passed the Taiwan Relations Act (TRA) to "declare that peace and stability in the Western Pacific are vital interests of the United States; the future of Taiwan should be determined by peaceful means; and that the United States will maintain the capacity to resist any use of force to change the status of Taiwan and provide Taiwan with arms of a defensive nature."[133]

The Taiwan Relations Act remains a very serious point of contention between the United States and China since this is in direct contradiction to the Chinese stated core interest of the national unity of China. As former Secretary of State and National Security Advisor Henry Kissinger has stated, "no issue preoccupies Chinese leaders more than the preservation of national unity."[134] Consequently, China's military remains focused on Taiwan with intent to develop "capabilities intended to deter, delay, or deny possible U.S. support for the island in the event of conflict. The balance of cross-Strait military forces and capabilities continues to shift in the mainland's favor."[135] Since the United States remains resolute to support the free and democratic nation of Taiwan, it justifies selling weapons to Taiwan for the following reasons: to enable Taiwan to defend itself (implying an attack by the PRC would be too costly in terms of

---

[133] David Lai, *Arms Sales to Taiwan: Enjoy the Business While It Lasts* (Carlisle Barracks: Strategic Studies Institute, May 2010), 2.

[134] Kissinger, *On China*, 523.

[135] DOD, *Annual Report to Congress*, 5.

military losses for the PLA), to enable Taiwan to defend itself for at least two weeks (with the planning assumption being it would take two weeks for an allied relief force to arrive), and to allow Taiwan to negotiate diplomatically with China from a position of strength.[136]

Taiwan also represents a geostrategic link in what is known as the "First Island Chain." The First Island Chain consists of the Korean Peninsula, Japan, the Ryuku Islands, Taiwan, the Philippines, Indonesia, and Australia. All of the countries, with the exception of North Korea, in the First Island Chain are democratic, and economic and defensive partners with the United States. From a Chinese perspective, this First Island Chain could be an American attempt at containment and is, therefore, undesired. If China were able to regain control of Taiwan, it would not only achieve the desire of a re-unified China, but from a security perspective it could break a vital link in the First Island Chain, denying the United States access to what General Douglas MacArthur called the "unsinkable aircraft carrier." Economically, regaining Taiwan would free up national assets, allowing China to use its energies to project power outward to a degree that has not been possible before. Robert Kaplan states, "It will be the fusing of Taiwan with the mainland that will mark the real emergence of a multi-polar world."[137]

How China and the United States Should Proceed in the Future

In his book, *On China*, Henry Kissinger writes that "The leaders on both sides of the Pacific have an obligation to establish a tradition of consultation and mutual respect so that, for their successors, jointly building a shared world order becomes an expression of parallel national aspirations."[138] He indicates that the relationship between the United States and China should be one of "co-evolution" that would allow each country to "identify and develop complementary interests" rather than looking at relations as a zero-sum game.[139] He cites one major source of tension being the perception each country has about the other. China is deeply concerned about the United States attempting to contain China. On

---

[136] Lai, *Arms Sales to Taiwan*, 2.
[137] Kaplan, *Monsoon*, 285.
[138] Kissinger, *On China*, 529.
[139] Ibid., 526.

the other hand, the United States is very concerned that China is attempting to "expel" the United States from Asia.[140]

For decades, especially during the Cold War, the United States maintained a policy of containment towards China. However, according to long time China watchers, Baogang and Sujian Guo, this policy was "inherently confrontational and hostile," even though it seemed logical due to the differences between the communist and liberal ideologies. [141] Dr. Yves-Heng Lim, another China scholar, also states that, "China's rise in the post-Cold War has transformed the U.S.-China relation into a quite perfect illustration of the classic contest between a dominant power and a rising challenger."[142] Containment and a balance-of-power approach to policy fall in the "realist" camp of international relations, but may not be the best way to proceed in the future.

There is also the political science theory of "complex interdependence" that basically states since there is such an economic interdependence between the United States and China, in which the two countries interests are intertwined, future relationships should be steered toward a direction of "mutual accommodation and cooperation."[143] International Relations professor, Pei-Shan Kao, has written that, "Complex interdependence does not necessarily lead to peace; however, it did and will continue to positively influence China-U.S. relations by making the use of force less likely and making their leaders consider their relations carefully and resolve their problems peacefully."[144] More pragmatic and moderate China observers tend to look at this condition of complex interdependence as a reason for China and the United States to seek symbiotic solutions to future problems.

---

[140] Ibid., 528.

[141] Guo, *Thirty Years of China-U.S. Relations*, 7.

[142] Yves-Heng Lim, "The Regional Logic of China-U.S. Rivalry" in *Thirty Years of China-U.S. Relations* (Plymouth, UK: Lexington Books, 2010), 50.

[143] Dennis Hickey and Yiran Zhou, "Chinese Mainland-U.S.-Taiwan Triangular Relations Since 2000: A Perspective of Complex Interdependence" in *Thirty Years of China-U.S. Relations* (Plymouth, UK: Lexington Books, 2010), 155.

[144] Pei-Shan Kao, "A Complex Interdependence: China-U.S. Relations" in *Thirty Years of China-U.S. Relations* (Plymouth, UK: Lexington Books, 2010), 111.

Former National Security Advisor, Zbingniew Brzezinski, recently addressed the relationship between China and the United States in his article "Balancing the East, Upgrading the West." He wrote that the United States and China should "exercise ideological self-restraint, resisting the temptation to universalize the distinctive features of their respective socioeconomic systems and demonize each other." By doing this, the two countries would reduce the possibility of conflict between each other, as well as lower the chance of possible miscalculations between China and its neighbors such as Japan, India, and Russia. He states that, "the United States must recognize that stability in Asia can no longer be imposed by a non-Asian power, least of all by the direct application of U.S. military power." He cautions against the United States establishing an "anti-Chinese" alliance with India, but ultimately suggests that for the near-term, the United States should follow a policy in Asia that upholds its obligations to "Japan and South Korea while not allowing itself to be drawn into a war between Asian powers on the mainland."[145] Brzezinski's article brings out a critical point for the United States to use self-restraint. It would be naïve and foolish for the United States to casually demonize China because of a different socioeconomic system.

America should consider China's long standing history with the West and the lessons from the Century of Humiliation. China is extremely distrustful of foreign powers and will go to great lengths to ensure its military can protect and defend China's territory. The United States must recognize this and respect this fact. It must also be sensitive to how a future military alliance with Russia or India would be seen as a possible threat to China's sovereignty. This is not to mean that the United States should ignore its defense treaties with Japan and South Korea, but the United States must know how far it is willing to go with military force projection. Instead, the United States should look for ways to work together with China on areas of mutual interest and benefit to the global commons.

---

[145] Zbignew Brzezinski, "Balancing the East, Upgrading the West," *Foreign Affairs* (January/February 2012), 102.

America's Pacific Century.

On 17 November 2011, President Barrack Obama announced, "Let there be no doubt: in the Asia-Pacific in the twenty-first century, the United States of America is all in."[146] This public statement announced the watershed moment for American diplomatic efforts by marking the shift of America's strategic focus from Europe to Asia. American Secretary of State, Hillary Clinton, reinforced the president's statement with an article "America's Pacific Century." In the article Clinton acknowledges that "the Asia-Pacific has become a key driver of global politics" and that the United States must remain engaged in the region in order to "sustain our leadership, secure our interests, and advance our values."[147] To do this, she outlined six lines of action:

> Strengthening bilateral security alliances
>
> Deepening our working relationships with emerging powers, including China
>
> Engaging with regional multilateral institutions
>
> Expanding trade and investment
>
> Forging a broad-based military presence
>
> Advancing democracy and human rights[148]

Regarding China, Secretary Clinton stated that the United States has worked hard to find areas of common interest, ways to build mutual trust, and encourage China's role and participation in global issues. Areas of mutual interest she identified were: North Korea, Afghanistan, Pakistan, Iran and developments in the South China Sea. However, she also identified areas and practices where China has been less than truthful. She wrote:

> We are working with China to end unfair discrimination against U.S. and other foreign companies or against their innovative technologies, remove preferences for domestic firms, and end measures that disadvantage or appropriate foreign intellectual property. And we look to China to take steps to allow its currency to appreciate more rapidly, both against the dollar and against the currencies of its other major trading partners.[149]

---

[146] *The Economist*, 19 November 2011, 43.

[147] Clinton, *America's Pacific Century*, 57.

[148] Ibid., 58

[149] Ibid., 60

Secretary Clinton's article depicts a pragmatic approach of dealing with China. It acknowledges the rise and importance of China on the global stage while still holding China accountable for actions that are seen as unfair or unappreciated by other international actors. By focusing on areas of mutual interest, the article demonstrates a desire by the United States to move forward with China in a positive direction although there may be issues where the two countries simply agree to disagree.

Conclusion.

The purpose of this monograph is to understand how China's culture affects the way it behaves internationally. By reviewing lessons from recent Chinese history and prevailing philosophies, and by applying the strategic lens described earlier, we can see that China has succeeded in their goal of achieving international recognition, both militarily and economically. However, the scars from the 'Century of Humiliation' run deep and will affect their future endeavors.

Expect China to continue to modernize their military, especially through weapon systems that provide them an advantage, such as ballistic missiles and submarines. These two weapon systems help counter the United State's direct military might and help level the playing field of a conventional conflict. However, the two areas China currently exploits to their advantage are information operations and cyberwarfare. Whether it is computer network attack, manipulation of satellite systems, or the disruption of computer networks, the Chinese appear to be ahead of the United States on ways leverage this new technology for military purposes. China will continue to invest heavily in cyberwarfare and asymmetric threats. This is currently the West's Achilles heel and a vulnerability that China will continue to exploit to their advantage. These aspects of warfare will be critical enablers in China's efforts to succeed in any anti-access and area denial capability that would be required in a military invasion of Taiwan from mainland China or in defense of North Korea. Using cyberwarfare and asymmetric threats also is in line with their characteristic principles of the indirect approach and timing. Asymmetric threats allow them to attack enemy weak points and vulnerabilities while the use of cyberwarfare enables them to develop, or create an imbalance that can be exploited to their advantage.

Any road to war, between China and the United States, will likely be caused by miscalculations. China will continue aggressive behavior and actions looking for opportunities to exploit in the Pacific. They will err by misreading the United States, or a defense treaty partner's actions (or inactions), as an opportunity to execute a move that could be perceived by the rest of the world as aggression. An example would be the sinking of a commercial vessel or the shooting down of a reconnaissance aircraft in a disputed territory zone. China might also test fire a ballistic missile that impacts in vicinity an American territory, such as Guam, or a territory of a defense treaty partner such as the Ryuku Islands of Japan (Okinawa).

The South China Sea will likely be used as a test bed to see how far China can push international treaties and how quickly, and strongly, neighboring countries might respond. Expect China to assume a more aggressive stance in the South China Sea once they have developed the naval and air capability of sustaining an enduring presence off shore. This would likely consist of multiple carrier strike groups for their navy and aerial refueling and early warning capabilities for their air force. China's justification for any military action would be reclaiming territory that they believe is rightfully theirs. Their demand for resources to sustain their economic growth would be the driving force behind any action.

Regarding Taiwan, China will continue their pursuit to unify Taiwan with the mainland; however, the use of force to achieve this unity is not likely in the immediate future. Given China's interdependence with the global economy, and high probability of significant losses on all sides if (Chinese, Taiwanese, and American) a conflict erupted, make the likelihood of a war over Taiwan unlikely. Any victory the Chinese might achieve would be Pyrrhic in nature and would likely result in the destruction of Taiwan's economic infrastructure which is one of the reasons the PRC's desire for unity.

It is clear that the CCP desires to remain in power and will take extraordinary steps to stay there. The party needs stability in order to perpetuate the regime and the best way to do this is through a strong economy. With a strong economy, the party can continue to placate the people enough to maintain their expectations and suppress civil unrest. However, a strong economy will not be possible without resources, and this need for more resources will drive China's foreign policy. China has developed their

56

'string of pearls' strategy and will likely stay on this course for the foreseeable future. Whether the United States agrees with this or particularly likes this policy is not the issue. The issue is what type of relationship the United States should have with China.

The United States has the global obligation to remain engaged with China and continue to encourage China to accept a regional leadership role on areas of mutually beneficial interest such as: playing a leading role in negotiations with the PRDK; participating in counter-piracy operations in both the Indian Ocean and the Straits of Malacca; supporting diplomatic efforts in counter-proliferation of nuclear materials (to include weapons); promoting and practicing responsible business practices; and developing the capability to participate in Humanitarian Assistance and Disaster Relief operations.

In the mean time, taking a lesson from China's strategic principles, while remaining engaged with China, the United States should let the situation develop over time with two things in mind. First, militarily, the United States should encourage military-to-military engagements in order to maintain channels for communication and build stronger personal relations; it should continue military exercises in the region to maintain its military capability and demonstrate resolve and support for our key allies, such as South Korea, Japan, and Australia. Secondly, diplomatically, the United States should reinforce its focus on the Asia-Pacific with renewed engagements with the Association of Southeast Asian Nations (ASEAN) and explore other regional relationships, with countries such as Burma and Vietnam, to ensure options are kept open.

The United States must acknowledge that the conditions on the international stage are changing very rapidly and should refrain from trying to apply an outdated, or cookie-cutter approach when dealing with China. At the same time, China's growing military capability cannot be ignored. The enduring strategic principles of the indirect approach, timing, and adaptability should be applied when considering Chinese intentions. Given these principles, the Chinese propensity for secrecy, and what is at stake for the nation, the way ahead for the United States can best be summed up by paraphrasing a quote from the Central Intelligence Agency, "In God we trust, all others we monitor."

APPENDIX

Twelve main articles of the Treaty of Nanjing.[150]

Article 1. Stipulated peace and friendship between Britain and China, and "full security and protection for their persons and property within the dominions of the other."

Article 2. Determined the opening of five Chinese cities—Canton, Fuzhou, Xiamen, Ningbo, and Shanghai—to residence by British subjects and their families 'for the purpose of carrying on their mercantile pursuits, without molestation or restraint.' It also permitted the establishment of consulates in each of the cities.

Article 3. 'The Island of Hong Kong to be possessed in perpetuity' by Victoria and her successors, and ruled as 'they shall see fit.'

Article 4. Payment of $6 million by the Qing 'as the value of the opium which was delivered up in Canton.'

Article 5. Abolition of the Canton Cohong monopoly system and permission at the five above-named ports for British merchants 'to carry on their mercantile transactions with whatever persons they please.' The Qing were to pay $3 million in settlement of outstanding Cohong debts.

Article 6. Payment to the British of a further $12 million 'on account of expenses incurred' in the recent fighting, minus any sums already received 'as a ransom for cities and towns in China' since August 1841.

Article 7. The $21 million stipulated in Article 4 through 6 were to be paid in four installments before the end of 1845, with a 5 percent interest charge per annum on late payments.

Article 8. Immediate release of any prisoner who were British subjects, whether Indian or European.

---

[150] Spence, *The Search for Modern China*, 158.

Article 9. An unconditional amnesty for all Chinese subjects who had resided with, dealt with, or served the British.

Article 10. At the five treaty ports listed in Article 2, all merchants should pay 'a fair and regular Tariff of Export and Import Customs and other Dues.' Once those fees were paid, only fair and stipulated transit dues should be paid on goods conveyed to the interior of China.

Article 11. Instead of terminology such as 'petition' or 'beg' that foreigners had previously been forced to use, nonderogatory and nonsubordinate terms of address such as 'communication,' ' statement,' and 'declaration' were to be used in future official correspondence between Britain and China.

Article 12. On receiving the first installment of the indemnity money, British forces would leave Nanjing and the Grand Canal, and 'no longer molest or stop the trade of China.' Troops would continue to hold Zhoushan until all money was paid and the 'opening [of] the Ports to British merchants be completed.'

BIBLIOGRAPHY

Secondary Sources

Beaver, R. Pierce. *Eerdman's Handbook to The World's Religions*. Edited by R. Peirce Beaver, et al. Grand Rapids, Michigan: Wm. B. Eerdmans Publishing Co. 1982.

Clausewitz, Carl von. *On War*. Translated and edited by Michael Howard and Peter Paret. New York: Alfred A. Knopf, 1984.

Craig, Susan L. *Chinese Perceptions of Traditional and Nontraditional Security Threats*. Carlisle Barracks: Strategic Studies Institute, March 2007.

Davies, Eryl. *Encyclopedia of Discovery Science and History*. Edited by Earl Davies, et al. San Francisco, California: Fog City Press, 2002.

Deng, Yong and Fei-Lei Wang., ed. *In the Eyes of the Dragon: China's Views of the World*. Lanham, Maryland: Rowman and Littlefield Publishers, Inc. 1999.

Dobbins, James, David C. Gompert, Andrew Scobell, and David A. Shlapak. *Conflict with China: Prospects, Consequences, and Strategies for Deterrence*. Santa Monica, California: Rand Corporation, 2011.

Dreyer, June Teufel. *China's Strategic View: The Role of the People's Liberation Army*. Carlisle Barracks: Strategic Studies Institute, April 1996.

Dupuy, R. Ernest and Trevor N. Dupuy. *The Encyclopedia of Military History, from 3500 B.C. to the Present*. New York: Harper and Row, Publishers, 1977.

Esposito, John L., Darrell J. Fasching, and Todd Lewis. *World Religions Today*. Oxford: Oxford University Press, 2002.

Fairbank, John K. *The United States and China, 4th ed.* Cambridge, Massachusetts: Harvard University Press, 1979.

Finkelstein, David M. and Kristen Gunness, ed. *Civil-Military Relations in Today's China: Swimming in a New Sea*. London: M. E. Sharpe, Inc., 2007.

Graff, David A. and Robin Higham. *A Military History of China*. Boulder, Colorado: Westview Press, 2002.

Guo, Sujian and Baogang Guo, ed. *Thirty Years of China-U.S. Relations*. Plymouth, UK: Lexington Books, 2010.

Harrison, Lawrence E., and Samuel P. Huntington, ed., *Culture Matters: How Values Shape Human Progress*. New York: Basic Books, 2000.

Hau, Yufan, C.X. George Wei, and Lowell Dittmer, ed. *Challenges to Chinese Foreign Policy: Diplomacy, Globalization, and the Next World Power*. Lexington: University of Kentucky Press, 2009.

Higgins, Lawrence D. "Modernization and Expansion of Japan," in *Brassey's Encyclopedia of Military History and Biography*. Washington: Brassey's Inc., 2000.

Jijun, Lieutenant General Li. *Traditional Military Thinking and the Defensive Strategy of China*. Carlisle Barracks: Strategic Studies Institute, August 1997.

Jordan, Donald A. *The Northern Expedition: China's National Revolution of 1926-1928*. Honolulu: The University of Hawaii Press, 1976.

Jullien, Francois. *A Treatise on Efficacy: Between Western and Chinese Thinking*. Honolulu: University of Hawaii Press, 2004.

Kaplan, Robert D. *Monsoon: The Indian Ocean and the Future of American Power*. New York: Random House, 2010.

Keith, Ronald C. *China: From the Inside Out*. New York: Pluto Press, 2009.

Kissinger, Henry. *On China*. New York: Penguin Press, 2011.

Lai, David. *Learning from the Stones: a GO Approach to Mastering China's Strategic Concept, Shi*. Carlisle Barracks: Strategic Studies Institute, May 2004.

_____. *China's Maritime Quest*. Carlisle Barracks: Strategic Studies Institute, June 2009.

_____. *Arms Sales to Taiwan: Enjoy the Business While It Lasts*. Carlisle Barracks: Strategic Studies Institute, May 2010.

Liang, Colonel Qiao and Colonel Wang Xiangsui. *Unrestricted Warfare: China's Master Plan to Destroy America*. Panama City, Panama: Pan American Publishing Company, 2002.

Lieberthal, Kenneth. *Governing China: From Revolution to Reform, Second Edition*. New York: W. W. Norton and Company, 2004.

Liu, Guoli, ed. *Chinese Foreign Policy in Transition*. New York: Aldine de Gruyter, 2004.

Louie, Kam, ed. *The Cambridge Companion to Modern Chinese Culture*. Cambridge: Cambridge University Press, 2008.

McGregor, Richard. *The Party: The Secret World of China's Communist Rulers*. New York: Harper Collins Publishers, 2010.

Mosher, Steven W. *Hegemon: China's Plan to Dominate Asia and the World*. San Francisco: Encounter Books, 2000.

Mott IV, William H. and Jae Chang Kim. *The Philosophy of Chinese Military Culture*. New York: Palgrave MacMillan, 2006.

Pye, Lucian. *China: An Introduction*. Boston: Little, Brown and Company, 1972.

Rees, David. "Red Star in the East," in *War in Peace, Conventional and Guerrilla Warfare Since 1945*. New York: Harmony Books, 1981.

Rogers, Lester B., Fay Adams, Walker Brown. *Story of Nations*. New York: Holt, Rinehart and Winston, Inc., 1962.

Sawyer, Ralph D. *Sun Tzu: The Art of War*. Boulder: Westview Press, 1994.

Scobell, Andrew. *China and Strategic Culture*. Carlisle Barracks: Strategic Studies Institute, May 2002.

Shambaugh, David. *Modernizing China's Military*. Berkeley, California: University of California Press, 2002.

Sheridan, James E. *China in Disintegration: The Republican Era in Chinese History, 1912-1949*. New York: The Free Press, A Division of Macmillan Publishing Co. Inc. 1975.

Snow, Edgar. *Red Star over China*. New York: Grove Press, 1961.

Spence, Jonathan D. *The Search for Modern China*. New York: W. W. Norton and Company, 1990.

Sutter, Robert G. *China's Rise in Asia.* Lanham, Maryland: Rowman and Littlefield Publishers, INC., 2005.

_____. *China's Rise in Asia-Promise, Prospects and Implications for the United States.* Honolulu: Asia-Pacific Center for Security Studies, February 2005.

Wang, Yuan-Kang. *Harmony and War: Confucian Culture and Chinese Power Politics.* New York: Columbia University Press, 2011.

Wasserstrom, Jeffrey N. *China in the 21st Century.* New York: Oxford University Press, 2010.

Zedong, Mao. *On Guerrilla Warfare.* Translated by Samuel B. Griffith II. Chicago: University of Illinois Press, 1961.

Zhu, Zhiqun. *US-China Relations in the 21st Century: Power in Transition and Peace.* London: Routledge, 2006.

Journals and Periodicals

Brzezinski, Zbignew. "Balancing the East, Upgrading the West." *Foreign Affairs* (January/February 2012): 97-104.

Coonen, Steve. "The Empire's Newest New Clothes: Overrating China." *Joint Forces Quarterly*, Issue 63, 4th Edition (2011): 84-91.

Central Intelligence Agency, "World Fact Book," https://www.cia.gov/library/publications/the-world-factbook/geos/ch.html (accessed December 9, 2011).

Clinton, Hillary. "America's Pacific Century." *Foreign Policy* (November 2011): 56-63.

Davis, Elizabeth Van Wie. "Governance in China in 2010." *Asian Affairs: An American Review* (2009): 195-211.

Department of Defense. "Annual Report to Congress on Military and Security Developments Involving the People's Republic of China." Washington, D.C. 6 May 2011.

Gertz, Bill. "China Supremacy." *The Washington Times*, November 23, 2011.

Hale, David D. and Lyric Hughes Hale. "Reconsidering Revaluation: The Wrong Approach to the U.S.-Chinese Trade Imbalance." *Foreign Affairs* (January/February 2008).

Ikenberry, G. John. "The Rise of China and the Future of the West." *Foreign Affairs* (January/February 2008).

Kaplan, Robert D. "The Geography of Chinese Power." *Foreign Affairs*, May/June 2010.

Larson, Daniel S. "U.S-China Relations: No Need to Fight." *Joint Forces Quarterly*, Issue 63, 4th Quarter (2011): 92-94.

Morrison, Wayne M. "China-U.S. Trade Issues." *Congressional Research Service*, September 30, 2011.

Shambaugh, Dr. David and Senior Colonel Wang Zhongchun. *China's Transition into the 21st Century: U.S. and PRC Perspectives.* Carlisle Barracks: Strategic Studies Institute, July 1996.

University of Texas, "University of Texas Map Library," http://lib.utexas.edu/maps/cia11/china_sm_2011.gif (accessed 22 January22, 2012).

Walgreen, David. "China in the Indian Ocean Region: Lessons in PRC Grand Strategy." *Comparative Strategy*, 2006: 55-73.

www.ingramcontent.com/pod-product-compliance
Lightning Source LLC
Chambersburg PA
CBHW081856280526
45789CB00007B/2729